Dictionary of Saints

BROCKHAMPTON PRESS
LONDON

This edition published 1996 by Brockhampton Press,
a member of the Hodder Headline PLC Group

ISBN 1 86019 331 6

2 4 6 8 10 9 7 5 3

Printed and bound in the UK

Introduction

The dictionary defines a saint as 'a person who, after death, is formally recognized by a branch of the Christian church, especially the Roman Catholic Church, as having attained, through holy deeds or behaviour, a specially exalted place in Heaven entitling him or her to veneration'. The word 'saint' comes from the Latin *sanctus*, meaning 'holy'. Early references were to saints generally (rather than to individuals), and those were taken to be all those faithful to the teachings of Jesus Christ. Later, the term came to be applied to categories, such as martyrs and the early monks. Martyrs were men and women who had suffered greatly in the service of Christ. They had lived lives of devotion, as well as of austerity and mortification. Often they had been tortured and executed because of their faith. It was the custom for the faithful to congregate at the place of martyrdom on the anniversary when the individual saint was honoured with rejoicing and feasting—hence 'feast day'. Gradually, it was applied to individuals, almost as an official title that went with a particular post, such as bishop, and finally acquired its meaning as defined above. It is necessary for a man or woman to be 'canonized' before he or she can properly be venerated as a saint. The term derives from the name being added to a 'canon' or list. Originally, individuals were recognized as saints by popular consent. Later, bishops gave permission for feasts to be held in honour of people, thereby 'canonizing' them. Later still, the process became the prerogative of the pope in Rome, and since the seventeenth century, has been very much more formal and rigorous than previously.

A

Adalbert [956–997]

St Adalbert was born in Bohemia and became bishop of Prague when he was only twenty-seven. His austerity angered his fellow Bohemians, who had only recently been converted, and he was forced to flee his diocese. He travelled to Rome where he remained for five years. Adalbert did return to Prague, but left again soon afterwards to carry the Gospel to the Hungarians. He also preached, although without much success, to the Poles and the Prussians. He was martyred in 997. His body was taken to the cathedral at Gnesen, and later to his native Prague. In 1880, his bones were discovered in a vault and his remains were re-interred in the cathedral. His feast day is 23 April.

Adamnan [c. 625–704]

St Adamnan was born in Ulster, in the part that is now Donegal. He joined the Columban brotherhood of Iona when he was twenty-eight, becoming abbot in 679. Seven years later, when visiting a former pupil, Aidfrid, king of Northumbria, to secure the release of some Irish prisoners, he was converted to the Roman view regarding the date of Easter, a view that he tried unsuccessfully to introduce to the Iona community. He had more success in Ireland. Adamnan wrote, in Latin, a treatise on the holy places of Palestine and other countries, which he claimed was dictated to him by Arculfus, a Frankish bishop who had been shipwrecked in the Western Isles when returning from a pilgrimage. This is one of the earliest written descriptions of Palestine. Adamnan is probably best known for his *Life of St Columba*, which, along with incredible stories and descriptions of miracles, contains remarkably detailed information about the community on Iona to which COLUMBA and Adamnan both belonged. Much knowledge of the early Scottish-Irish church has been gleaned from this work. His feast day is 23 September.

Adelaide of Burgundy [*c*. 931–999]
St Adelaide, already widow of Lothair, king of Italy, married the emperor Otto the Great and was crowned empress by Pope John XII in 962. After Otto died in 973, Adelaide was badly treated by both her son and grandson, and she had to leave the court for a time. She served as regent but found the burden too great. Adelaide founded a convent in Alsace, where she died. Her feast day is 16 December.

Adrian of Canterbury [died 710]
St Adrian was born in Africa. When he was abbot of Nerida, he was offered the archbishopric of Canterbury by Pope St Vitalian. When he declined this post, Adrian was instructed by the pope to travel to England with the new archbishop, THEODORE, who was a Greek monk. When they eventually reached Canterbury, Adrian was installed in the abbey that became St AUGUSTINE's. He became an influential teacher,

being particularly esteemed as a scholar of Greek and Latin. He was buried in his own monastery. His feast day is 9 January.

Aegidius *see* **Giles**.

Aelfheah *see* **Alphege**.

Agatha [died 251]

St Agatha was born in Sicily. She belonged to a noble and wealthy family and was famous for her beauty and gentleness. Although she was greatly admired by the governor, Quintianus, she had already resolved to dedicate her life to Christ. Her refusal of Quintianus' approaches resulted in Agatha's being put on trial and tortured, from which treatment she finally died. She is the patron saint of bell-founders. Symbolic emblems in depictions of Agatha include tongs and shears (her torture), a veil, and a flaming building. Her feast day is 5 February.

Agnes [died 303]

St Agnes was a Roman who died when she was only thirteen, having suffered under the persecution of the Christians ordered by the Roman emperor Diocletian. Although she is one of the most famous of the Roman martyrs, very little is known about her. She was rich and beautiful and had many suitors, including the son of the prefect of the city. She rejected his advances, however, on the grounds that she was already 'espoused' to Christ. She was sentenced to be driven naked into a house of ill repute where, it is said, she was pursued by her lover. She was protected by angels from any assault by him. She was condemned to be burned, but she prayed and the fire went out. She was killed by being stabbed in the throat with a sword. Agnes is usually represented with a lamb (which is her emblem), or a sword, an olive branch, a crown of olives, a flaming pyre, and with an angel protecting her. Her feast day is 21 January.

Aidan [died 651]

St Aidan was an Irish Scot and a monk of Iona. He founded the Northumbrian church. In 635, Oswald, king of Northumbria, requested that a missionary be sent from Iona to evangelize his kingdom. The missionary returned and declared that the Northumbrians were so stubborn and barbaric that he had been able to do nothing. Aidan expressed the view that the missionary had been too direct and unrelenting in his approach. His brethren were so impressed that Aidan was consecrated bishop and was sent to Oswald to have a go himself. He made his base on the island of Lindisfarne. With the help of the king and several Irish missionaries, much progress was made. Churches were built and monasteries established. Aidan travelled extensively, almost always on foot. It is said that he did not hesitate to rebuke the haughty and the powerful, but was tender when comforting the afflicted and defending the poor. Much time was spent reading the Scriptures and learning Psalms. Aidan introduced the custom of fasting until 3 o'clock in the afternoon on Wednesdays and Fridays throughout the year, except during the forty days after Easter. Many miracles were attributed to Aidan. One of the best known concerned a priest named Utta who was to travel to Kent by sea and asked Aidan to pray for him. Aidan prophesied a storm and gave Utta some oil, telling him to cast it upon the waves when the storm broke. As prophesied, a storm overwhelmed the ship and all had given up hope when Utta poured the oil on the waters and the storm abated. He is also credited with saving the royal city of Bamburgh from fire. Aidan was struck down by illness in 651 after he had been bishop for sixteen years. His body was taken to Lindisfarne and buried there. He was greatly admired by BEDE for his holy, loving and apostolic life. His feast day is 31 August.

Alban [died *c.* 304]

St Alban was the first English martyr and very little is known about him. In 429, St GERMAN or Germanus of Auxerre visited Verulam (modern-day St Albans) and worshipped in a little church that held the remains of Alban, a martyr. When Germanus returned to France, he took back with him some bloodstained earth as a relic. The date of Alban's martyrdom is uncertain, although it is said to have happened during the persecution of Diocletian around 304–305. The account by Bede suggests that Alban, then a pagan, gave shelter to a priest who was fleeing from persecution, perhaps under a local Roman governor. The priest converted Alban to Christianity. When the priest's pursuers tracked him down to Alban's house and demanded that he be handed over, Alban put on the priest's clothes and gave himself up. When he refused to renounce his Christianity, he was sentenced to be beheaded. On his way to be executed, Alban and his tormentors could not cross a river as the bridge was crowded with spectators. Alban prayed and the river dried up. At his place of execution, on a hill, Alban again prayed, and this time a spring emerged under his feet. His executioner was so moved that he threw down his sword, refused to execute Alban and threw himself at Alban's feet. Another soldier had to be called, and he executed both men. A church was built on the site of Alban's martyrdom, on what is known as Holy Well Hill. That church was superseded by the abbey church of St Albans, built by Offa, king of Mercia, in 793. His feast day is 20 June.

Alberic [died 1109]
Also known as Aubrey, St Alberic was one of the founders of the mother house of the Cistercian order. With other, like-minded monks, Alberic settled at Citeaux in Burgundy in 1098, and Alberic became abbot the following year. He set an example of hard work and poverty, and the house he founded became the basis of one of the most influential religious orders. His feast day is 26 January.

Albert the Great [1206–1280]
St Albert was born in Swabia in southern Germany. After studying at the University of Padua, he joined the Order of Preachers and taught as a theologian in several parts of Germany before making Cologne his headquarters in 1248. St THOMAS AQUINAS was one of his students. He taught Scripture in Rome and became bishop of Regensburg in 1260, but returned to teaching two years later. Albert was a prolific writer, covering a wide range of subjects, and is sometimes called the 'Universal Teacher'. He was canonized by Pope

Pius XI in 1931. He is the patron saint of students of natural sciences. His feast day is 15 November.

Aldhelm [*c*. 640–709]
Also known as Ealdhelm, St Aldhelm was born in Wessex and became abbot of Malmesbury around 673 and bishop of Sherborne in 705. He was a skilled architect and built a church at Bradford-on-Avon, which some believe still stands, although others identify the present building as a later, tenth-century successor. Aldhelm was a renowned scholar who wrote Latin treatises, letters and verses (including riddles). He is known to have written verse in English, but his poems have not survived. He was buried at Malmesbury abbey. His feast day is 25 May.

Alexander Nevsky [1219–1263]
St Alexander Nevsky was the son of the grand duke Jaroslav of Novgorod who was forced to submit to Mongol domination in 1238. In 1240, Alexander scored a famous victory over the Swedes on the River Neva (from which he is named), near to where St Petersburg now stands. He succeeded his father in 1247 and stood out against a papal attempt to reunite the Greek and Roman churches. To the end of his life he remained a vassal of the Tartars, or Mongols, but he was skilled in moderating their tyranny and was known as a good prince. Peter the Great honoured his memory by building a magnificent convent on the site of his victory and by founding the knightly order of Alexander Nevsky. He was canonized by the Russian Orthodox church in 1547. He was the subject of a famous Russian film di-

rected in 1938 by Eisenstein with music by Prokofiev. His feast day is 23 November.

Alexis [fifth century]

St Alexis was known as the 'Man of God'. He is reputed to have died a nameless beggar, despite being the son of a Roman patrician. The medieval legend of Alexis has it that he married but left his wife on their wedding day and went to live in poverty in Syria. Later he returned to his father's house where he lived unrecognized as a servant and slept under the stairs until his death many years after that. He was the patron saint of a society of nurses known as the Alexian Brothers. In art he is often represented by a beggar with a bowl, or as a poor pilgrim, and also by the emblem of the martyr's palm. His feast day is 17 July.

Aloysius [1568–1591]

St Aloysius was born Luigi Gonzaga near Brescia in Italy, the eldest son of the marquis of Castiglione. He studied in Florence, Mantua and Rome, and the intention was that he should become a soldier. However, Aloysius was not attracted to the typical life of the nobleman of his day, and he renounced his entitlement to be marquis in favour of his brother and joined the Society of Jesus (the Jesuits) in 1585, overcoming his father's strong disapproval. During a plague epidemic, Aloysius devoted himself to caring for the sick and himself succumbed to the disease and died at the age of only twenty-three. He was canonized in 1726. His feast day is 21 June.

Alphege [954–1012]

Also known as **Aelfheah**, St Alphege entered the monastery
of Deerhurst in Gloucestershire, then at Bath, and, having attracted the attention of St DUNSTAN, who was archbishop of
Canterbury, was appointed bishop of Winchester in 984
when he was barely thirty. Ten years later, the Danes and
Norwegians were overrunning the east and south of England,
and King Ethelred was helpless. Alphege had heard that the
king of Norway had been baptised in the Scilly Isles and persuaded Ethelred to send him as envoy to Olaf, who was persuaded by Alphege to make peace with the English king. In
1005, Alphege was made archbishop of Canterbury. When
he returned from Rome, England was still subject to maraud-
ing raids by the Danes. Alphege instigated a number of reforms in a spirit of national penitence for sins that had
brought the 'wrath of heaven' on the nation. But the reforms
came too late, and the Danes besieged Canterbury in 1010,
when they were bought off, and again in 1011. Alphege was
advised to flee but he refused and became a mainstay of the
defence. But the defence was in vain—Canterbury was
sacked and the cathedral burned. The archbishop was taken
prisoner. He was taken to London and held for seven months,
demanding a ransom for his life. Alphege refused to allow a
ransom to be paid, believing that his people had suffered
enough. During his imprisonment, Alphege was not idle. He
ministered to the soldiers who held him and even confirmed
one of them. On the Sunday after Easter 1012, the Danes
went ashore at Greenwich, got drunk and renewed their demand for a ransom for Alphege. Again he refused and, in a
rage, the soldiers pelted him with ox bones and horns until

one soldier, taking pity on him, put him to death with an axe. His feast day is 19 April.

Ambrose [340–397]

St Ambrose was born at Trèves where his father was the Roman prefect of Gaul (modern-day France). When he was in his cradle, a swarm of bees settled round his mouth but did not sting him. His father, who had heard of a similar event in the life of Plato, regarded this as a good omen and believed that it foretold a great destiny for Ambrose. The boy received a first-class education and went with his brother to Milan to study law. He so distinguished himself that, at the age of only twenty-nine, he was appointed prefect of Upper Italy and Milan. His gentleness and wisdom won for him the affection of the people, to such an extent that there was a unanimous call for him to be made bishop of Milan in 374. For a long time, Ambrose resisted and even left the city. But he soon returned, was baptised, and was consecrated bishop on 7 December. Ambrose sold his belongings and distributed the proceeds among the poor. He then undertook a course of theological study to equip himself for his new role. As bishop, although kind and gentle, he could also be severe, and he condemned wickedness, even in high places. He barred the emperor Theodosius from the church because he had ordered a massacre at Thessalonica in which seven thousand people perished, and excommunicated him. Theodosius was not restored to communion until he had done public penance and had promised that no one should be executed until thirty days after sentence had been passed. Ambrose's most valuable legacy to the church are his hymns and the modifications that he introduced to worship. His symbolic emblems include a beehive, a three-knotted scourge and a whip. He is the patron saint of Milan. His feast day is 7 December.

Andrew [first century]

St Andrew was the first apostle to be called by Jesus. He belonged to Galilee and was the brother of Simon Peter. John's Gospel tells us that Andrew was one of the two disciples of St JOHN THE BAPTIST who heard him say of Christ, 'Behold, the Lamb of God' and at once followed Jesus. His first act was to find his brother Simon and bring him too to Jesus. He may also have been instrumental in bringing St PHILIP, who was of the same city. At the feeding of the five thousand, it was Andrew who told Jesus about the boy who had the loaves and the fishes. And John tells us that, when the Greeks wanted to see Jesus, they approached St Philip and St Andrew. According to tradition, Andrew was the first to preach the gospel in Russia, where he is greatly revered. Another tradition holds that he preached in Achaia, a province of ancient Greece, where he converted the wife of the Roman proconsul, who ordered that Andrew should be scourged and bound to a cross—not nailed, so that his death might be more lingering. Andrew is said to have preached from the cross to twenty thousand men and that he took two days to die. Many of those who heard him were converted. Andrew's body was taken to Constantinople by the emperor Constantine. Andrew is associated with Scotland, of which he is patron saint. St Rule (or Regulus) was charged to take care of the relics of St Andrew. In a dream, he was warned by an angel to take them to a place yet to be named. Eventually he found his way to a spot that later came to be called St Andrews and there he deposited the relics. Andrew is also the patron saint of Greece and Russia. His main emblem is the cross in the shape of an X, or saltire, but he is also often depicted with a net containing fish, or a length of rope (as he was bound to the cross). His feast day is 30 November.

Anne [first century BC]

St Anne was the mother of the Virgin MARY. She is first mentioned in Christian literature in the fourth century AD. She is said to have been the wife of a rich man called Joachim and, for many years, bore no children. One year, when Anne and Joachim came to the temple for the festival of dedication, Joachim was upbraided by the priest for having fathered no children. Cut to the heart, and not able to face the scorn of his neighbours, Joachim went into the wilderness for forty days and gave himself up to prayer. Meanwhile Anne remained in Jerusalem. Each had a vision of angels promising them a daughter, who would be called Mary and who was to be dedicated to God from the moment of her birth. Anne is often depicted in a red robe covered by a green cloak, green symbolizing rebirth and red standing for love. Many miracles were attributed to St Anne in the Middle Ages, but her festival was not observed until the sixteenth century. Her feast day is 26 July.

Anselm [1033–1109]

St Anselm was born at Aosta, the son of a rich Lombard of rank. He was a devout and studious child and at the age of sixteen wanted to become a monk, but his father refused his permission. Anselm left home at the age of twenty-three and found his way to the abbey at Bec where he joined the order, succeeding Lanfranc as prior three years later. He was prior from 1063 to 1078 and abbot from 1078 to 1093. In these posts he was noted for his devoutness and asceticism. He was also affectionate and sympathetic to those around him. And he was a famous teacher. His affection extended to animals—he is said to have burst into tears when a hunted hare took refuge under the feet of his horse; he ordered that its life be protected. William the Conqueror, not known for his mild and gentle manner, fell under Anselm's spell and, when he lay dying at Rouen, sent for the monk to hear his last confession. Anselm was a frequent visitor to England and was well known to the high and mighty in the land. In 1092, he was (despite his protestations) unexpectedly appointed archbishop of Canterbury by the dying William Rufus, the staff was forced into his hand and he was carried aloft to the cathedral. Thereafter, Anselm's life was one of endless strife. He had to put up a strong and determined independence against both William and Henry I. And, although abandoned by the bishops, he resolutely maintained his right to acknowledge Urban II as pope. He refused to give in to the king's financial demands and rebuked the monarch for his sins—William's immorality was a source of great anguish to Anselm. But nothing would deflect Anselm from what he knew to be right. The king continued, with the support of the council and bishops, to try to persuade Anselm to forfeit his recognition of Urban as pope. After four years of fruitless controversy, Anselm decided he could do no more good in

England and travelled to Rome to seek advice and protection. While there, he completed his treatise on the Incarnation, *Cur Deus Homo*. When he heard the news that William Rufus had been killed, he returned hastily to England, where he immediately encountered difficulties with Henry. Their dispute about old versus new practices of the church was finally brought to a compromise by the intervention of the pope in 1107. Anselm's life was now nearing its close. He continued diligently to discharge the duties of his office and in putting down abuses of all kinds. He maintained a constant correspondence with kings and princes as well as lesser folk who sought his advice. He died at the age of seventy-six and was buried in Canterbury next to Lanfranc. His body was later removed to the chapel that bears his name. His feast day is 21 April.

Antony of Padua [1195–1231]

St Antony was born at Lisbon in Portugal. He was first an Augustinian monk, but later joined the Franciscans and became one of the order's foremost propagators. He preached in southern France and northern Italy. He practised severe asceticism and vigorously opposed a move to relax the strictness of Franciscan rule. It is said that, when men refused to listen to him, he preached to the fishes. He is the patron saint of the lower orders of animals and is often represented accompanied by a kneeling ass. His emblems include a flaming heart, a flowered cross or crucifix, and the lily, the symbol of purity. His monument is in the church that bears his name at Padua. Antony was canonized by Pope Gregory IX in 1232. His feast day is 13 June.

Antony the Great [251–356]

St Antony was born in Egypt, the son of noble Christian parents who died when he was young and left him considerable wealth. He was a devout child and, on hearing the words of the Gospel, 'If thou wouldest be perfect, sell that thou hast, and give to the poor', he was so impressed that he gave away all he owned and became a hermit. He led a life of strict prayer and never ate more than once a day—sometimes only once in two days. His food was bread and salt, and he drank only water. He lay on the bare ground and worked with his hands. Despite these austerities, Antony was tempted by impure thoughts—it is said that the Devil appeared to him in the form of a beautiful woman, but Antony's virtue was proof against all temptation. When he was thirty-five, he went into the desert and hid himself underground. He remained there alone for twenty years. Twice a year, his friends brought him bread that they lowered into the cave. He had no other visitors, and it was thought that he passed most of his time in conflict with devils. Later, he returned to his former life and converted many people by word and example. Cells sprang up in the desert and were colonized by monks. Antony governed over them like a father, and some believe this to be the foundation of the monastic community as a way of life. During Maximian's persecution, Antony travelled to Alexandria and, although he longed for martyrdom, instead he ministered to the persecuted and comforted them in their confinement or on their way to execution. Once more, he retired to the desert but was continually interrupted by endless streams of people seeking his advice. He seldom thereafter left his cell, although he did again travel to Alexandria 'on one occasion. He is said to have banished the wild beasts from the desert and was believed to have the gift of second sight. Antony died at the age of 105, having commanded that his body be buried and not embalmed in the Egyptian manner. He was the greatest of the hermits and the founder of monasticism. He is often depicted accompanied by a pig (an animal that was bred by Antonine monks) with a bell hung around its neck to drive off evil spirits. His feast day is 17 January.

Athanasius [296–373]

St Athanasius was born in Alexandria in Egypt, where he was brought up by Alexander, the bishop of the city. He was a disciple of St ANTONY THE GREAT and may have been inspired by Antony in his asceticism. While he was still a young man, Athanasius wrote two treatises, *Against the Gentiles* and *On the Incarnation*. He became archdeacon and attended, with Alexander, a council of all the bishops of the Catholic church at Nicaea, assembled by the emperor to hear the heretic Arius. The council condemned Arius. Shortly afterwards, Alexander died, having nominated Athanasius as his successor. He was duly elected by the Egyptian bishops, and his election was approved by the laity of Alexandria. One of Athanasius' first acts as bishop was to organize the church in Abyssinia. Frumentius was consecrated bishop and returned to his native Abyssinia (now Ethiopia) to build up the Christian church there. Athanasius was in constant conflict with the followers of Arius, who denied the divinity of Christ. He was exiled at least four times, and every kind of charge, from immorality to murder, was levelled against

him. His life was constantly in danger. For six years he lived
with the Egyptian hermits in the desert. But Athanasius
never faltered, and it is to his credit that the Catholic church
retained its faith in the Lord, afterwards enshrined in the
Nicene Creed. He returned to Alexandria where he died in
373. His feast day is 2 May.

Aubrey *see* **Alberic**.

Audrey *see* **Etheldreda**.

Augustine of Canterbury [died 604]
Also known as **Austine**, St Augustine was prior at the monastery of St ANDREW in Rome when he was sent by Pope
GREGORY THE GREAT with a band of monks to convert the
English. They had not got far when word reached them of the
savageness of those they had been sent to convert. They sent
Augustine back to Rome to seek permission to abandon the
journey. But Gregory exhorted them to continue and, under
the protection of the Frankish rulers of Gaul, they completed
their journey, and landed on the island of Thanet in 597.
Ethelbert, king of Kent, had married the daughter of the king
of Paris. Bertha was a Christian and worshipped in the ancient church of St Martin. When Augustine sent envoys to
Ethelbert announcing that they came from Rome with 'a
message of great joy', the king was suspicious, fearing magi-
cal arts. He insisted that the messengers from Rome meet
him in an open field. Ethelbert was sufficiently persuaded of
their sincerity that he gave them permission to preach and to
win over as many of the population as they could. Augustine

and his companions lived in Canterbury, and they too used the church of St Martin. They soon won converts. Ethelbert himself was baptised and, although he compelled none to follow his example, the work of conversion was helped enormously. Augustine then went to Arles where he was consecrated 'bishop of the English'. He built a monastery on the site of an old Roman basilica, where the present cathedral now stands, and a church to St PETER and St PAUL on a site where St Augustine's College now stands. In 601, Gregory sent Augustine the pall (the small, square linen cloth with which the chalice is covered at the Eucharist) and a letter containing a plan for the organization of the English church. There were to be two archbishops, one in London and one in York, and each was to have twelve suffragans. Augustine himself was to be bishop of London. Two years later, Augustine convened a famous conference of the bishops of the ancient British church. He exhorted them to observe Catholic unity, that is, to renounce their distinctive traditions relating to the date of Easter and other matters, and to join him in preaching the Gospel to the heathen English. After long and fruitless argument, Augustine appealed to miracle. A blind man was presented and, after the British bishops had tried and failed to cure him of his blindness, St Augustine restored the man's sight. Even this was not quite enough to win over the bishops, who requested time to consult their followers and a second conference, which Augustine agreed to. At this new meeting, Augustine found the bishops recalcitrant. He finally offered to let them keep their ancient traditions, except for agreeing the date of Easter, baptism according to Roman custom, and preaching to the English. They refused, and the conference broke up with Augustine threatening divine judgment. St Augustine is belittled by some—partly on the grounds of lack of warmth and charm. But he was confronted with an immensely difficult task. He died before he had been in England seven years, and it says much for his apostolic life and labours that he achieved as much as he did. His feast day is 27 May (26 May in England).

Augustine of Hippo [354–430]

St Augustine was perhaps the greatest of the Latin fathers. He was the son of St MONICA, born in Numidia (approximately present-day Algeria) in North Africa. His mother taught him the Christian faith, although he was not baptised until some time later, as was the custom of the time. Augustine had a wild and stormy youth. Although passionate and intelligent, he was practically an infidel and was guilty of moral weakness and intellectual wilfulness. Through all this, however, the name of Christ remained firmly fixed in his mind. He went to Carthage to study rhetoric and read a treatise by Cicero that influenced him greatly. 'This book altered my plans and changed my purposes,' and afterwards Augustine was a seeker after truth, although his search was a long one. He read the Bible but found its style vulgar. He was also dismayed by the moral difficulties that it contained. He became entangled with the Manichaeans, who held, among other strange doctrines, that man's body was intrinsically evil. He found their creed unsatisfactory and soon moved on to Platonism. This too he found unsatisfactory. When he was twenty-nine, Augustine went to Rome, then two years later to Milan where he came under the influence of the bishop, St

AMBROSE. He listened to Ambrose preach every week, but continued to wrestle with the conflict between flesh and spirit. He found it difficult to give up his old, sinful ways. One day, he heard a voice as he lay under a fig tree. He saw no human speaker, so took this to be divine guidance exhorting him to read the Scriptures. He clearly chose the right part to read, as shortly afterwards, to the great joy of his mother, Monica, he was baptised in 387 when he was thirty-three. He became an ordained priest at Hippo in 391 and bishop in 395. As bishop, he was ascetic and severe in his habits but was generous towards the poor. He lived frugally in a monastery with his clergy. As a writer, he profoundly influenced Christian doctrine. For centuries, his was the prevailing influence in the western church. And in the sixteenth century, his writings were the quarry where the Reformers dug for their arguments. He came into conflict with the Donatists, who would deny the title Catholic to any church that admitted unworthy or lapsed members, and with a British monk, Pelagius, who denied man's need of divine grace. Augustine wrote many theological works, including *Confessions* and *De Civitate Dei*. His emblem is the flaming heart, and he is often depicted with arrows piercing his chest as a sign of his remorse for rejecting the bible as a student. His feast day is 28 August.

Austine *see* **Augustine of Canterbury**.

B

Barnabas [first century]
St Barnabas was born Joseph in Cyprus. The disciples gave him the name Barnabas, which means 'son of exhortation'. He may have been one of the seventy disciples, and is mentioned in the New Testament, in the book of Acts. When St PAUL first visited Jerusalem after his conversion and found that the disciples were afraid of him, Barnabas came forward and brought Paul to the apostles and spoke for him. Later Barnabas was sent on a mission from Jerusalem to Antioch where the disciples, scattered after the persecution that followed the death of St STEPHEN, were preaching to both Jews and Greeks. Barnabas sought out Paul and they taught together for a year. After this time, they went on what is generally taken to be Paul's first missionary journey, first visiting Barnabas' home, Cyprus. During this journey, Paul was taken for Mercury and Barnabas for Jupiter. They returned to Antioch to continue their work. A question arose about the need for gentile converts to be circumcised. The church at Antioch sent Barnabas and Paul to Jerusalem to consult the apostles and elders. When, around the year 48, Paul and Barnabas went their separate ways, Barnabas to Cyprus and Paul to Syria, history loses sight of Barnabas. Nothing more is known about his life, although there are various accounts

of his death. Some said he was stoned to death in Cyprus and his body removed to Constantinople. According to another account, his body was taken to Milan when the Saracens conquered Cyprus. Barnabas was a cousin of St MARK. His feast day is 11 June.

Bartholomew [first century]
St Bartholomew is usually identified with Nathanael, who is mentioned in the New Testament in the book of John. He appears also as one of the seven fisherman on the sea of Tiberias to whom Jesus appeared after the Resurrection. He was thought to have been of noble birth and to have preached in India where he was martyred by being flayed alive. He is often represented carrying the knife with which he was flayed, sometimes with the flayed skin carried in his hand or over his arm. His feast day is 24 August.

Basil [329–379]
Also called **Basil the Great**, St Basil was the son of wealthy parents, born at Caeserea, the capital of Cappadocia, an ancient region of east Asia Minor. He was educated at Caeserea, Constantinople and in Athens, and he attracted attention wherever he went through his talents and his virtuous life. In 356, he returned to his native city and became a teacher of rhetoric, was hugely popular and wore the graces of a man of fashion. When he was thirty, he resolved to be baptised and to renounce the world. He toured Egypt and Palestine, visiting the most celebrated ascetics of the day, seeking advice on how best to put his renunciation into ef-

fect. At Pontus, where he remained for five years, he was first to adopt the community system for monks, who had hitherto lived as solitaries. His rule combined industrious activity with devotion. St BENEDICT was greatly influenced by Basil. Only one meal a day, of bread, herbs and water, was permitted. Sleep was allowed only until midnight, when everyone rose to pray. In 370, Basil became bishop of Caeserea, whose office included also that of metropolitan of Cappadocia. He devoted the rest of his life to the restoration of orthodoxy and unity to the scattered fragments of the eastern church, although in failing health and in the face of jealousy and intrigue among those on whose support he should have been able to rely. He incurred the wrath of the Arian emperor and, despite threats, refused to communicate with the emperor's bishops and officials. Basil died, worn out, when he was fifty. He had written many theological treatises, including the Liturgy that bears his name. His feast day (with GREGORY NAZIANZENS) is 2 January.

Bede [673–735]

Known as the **Venerable Bede**, he was born in Northumbria and, aged seven, went to be educated in the Benedictine monastery of St Peter and St Paul at Wearmouth. He was studious and dutiful, becoming a deacon at the age of nineteen and a priest at thirty. He appears to have spent most of his life in the monastery and never to have ventured outside Northumberland. He wrote prolifically, and the most important of his more than forty works is an *Ecclesiastical History of the English People*. Bede has been called the 'father of English history'. When he was a child, all the monks died of plague except himself and one other. About two weeks before Easter in 735, he fell ill. Every hour he gave thanks to God, day and night, and remained in good spirits. When not praying or singing the offices, he read with his pupils. He translated part of the Gospel of St JOHN into English. As his condition worsened, he begged his scribe to write more quickly as he did not know how long he might last. When the boy announced that the text was finished, Bede was placed on the floor of his cell, where he chanted the Gloria until he died. There are several explanations of why Bede is called 'Venerable'. In one account, when he was blind at the end of his life, he was tricked into preaching to a pile of stones, which, when he had finished, cried out 'Amen, Venerable Bede'. In another, the epitaph on his tombstone was completed by an angel to include the word 'venerabilis'. A stone in Durham cathedral bears the same inscription. His feast day is 25 May.

Benedict [480–543]

St Benedict was born into a noble Roman family. At the age of fourteen, he renounced the world and went to live as a hermit in the mountains. On his way, he met a monk who gave Benedict a hair shirt and a habit made of skin. He found a rocky cave and lived there for three years. His fame spread, and people came to visit him in his cave. The monks of a neighbouring monastery persuaded Benedict to be their ruler, but they disliked his severity and tried to remove him with poison—when Benedict made the sign of the Cross over the cup containing the poison, it shattered into pieces. He went back to his cave, and so many disciples came to him there that he founded twelve monasteries, each inhabited by twelve monks. His enormous following made his brethren jealous, and attempts were made on both his virtue and his life. Ultimately he withdrew to Monte Cassino where he founded the order of Benedictines, which set the pattern for western monasticism for the next six hundred years. All other orders were affiliated to it or grew out of it. The Benedictine was the only recognized order until the establishment of the Dominicans and Franciscans. The principle that governed Benedict's order was separation from the world—a world in which the old civilizations were breaking up, a world of barbarian hordes and of fraud, force and violence. To those who wanted to follow Christ, flight from the world seemed the only path. They sought to be separated from worldly and carnal desires and be free to find Christ through prayer and meditation. And so they looked for solitary places, observed silence and worked with their hands to subdue the demands of the flesh. Benedict remained at Monte Cassino for fourteen years. He was renowned for his faith and charity—when a famine afflicted Campania in 539, Benedict distributed all the monastery's provisions to the poor, to the dismay of the monks. When the house was down to its last five loaves, Benedict rebuked the brothers for their lack of faith, and next morning two hundred bushels of flour were found at the gate. He died standing at the foot of the altar with his arms raised to heaven and uttering a final prayer. He is usually depicted with his finger touching his lip, as though enjoining silence, and with a rose bush or a disciple by his side. His emblems are a broken cup or pitcher, symbolizing the spilling of the poisoned wine, a broken sieve, a raven, symbolizing the raven that carried away poisoned bread with which a priest had planned to kill him, and a thorn bush (Benedict threw himself onto a thorn bush to distract himself from temptation. His feast day is 11 July.

Berin *see* **Birinus**.

Bernadette [1844–1879]
St Bernadette was born Bernadette Soubirous, the daughter of a miller at Lourdes in southern France. When she was fourteen, Bernadette saw a vision of the Virgin Mary, who told the girl that a spring lay below the ground. Many, especially the clergy, refused to believe Bernadette's account of events. Nevertheless, a spring was found and a shrine created to which many flocked seeking cures for disabilities and diseases. Bernadette joined the Sisters of Notre Dame at Nevers in 1866. After attracting much unwelcome attention in the world, she wished to escape to a life of duty and prayer. She died at the age of thirty-five and was canonized in 1933. Her feast day is 16 April.

Bernard of Clairvaux [1091–1153]
St Bernard was the son of a knight of Burgundy, born in his father's castle at Fontaines near Dijon. As a child, he was learned and thoughtful beyond his years. He abandoned his early ambition for a life of intellectual activity in favour of becoming a Cistercian monk at Citeaux when he was twenty-two. He had such influence even then that he persuaded an uncle and four brothers, one of whom was married with children, to follow his example. Bernard preached and urged people to renounce the world, with some success—it is said

he turned up at the abbey gates with thirty converts. The monastery kept the strict rule of St BENEDICT, the monks eating only one meal a day and that not until twelve hours after rising. Even this regime was too easy for Bernard who found ways of adding further austerities. After two years, he was chosen by the abbot to found a daughter house. In 1115, he took twelve monks and set up a rudimentary house in a valley in Langres, and this was the beginning of the famous house of Clairvaux. At first the monks suffered appalling hardship, and it was only Bernard's faith and courage that prevented them from giving up in despair. Before long the monastery was securely established. Bernard spent most of the next fifteen years at Clairvaux, where he preached, studied and taught. His fame spread throughout Europe, and many wrote to him for advice. He did not hesitate to remonstrate with a wrongdoer, even if that person were the abbot of Cluny or the king of France. In 1130, the papacy was the subject of a dispute between Innocent II and an antipope who called himself Anacletus II. St Bernard spoke for Innocent's claim, even petitioning the kings of France and England and the Holy Roman emperor. His success made him one of the most powerful men in Europe. Popes and kings sought his advice and support. His monks occupied the most prestigious sees—one became archbishop of Canterbury, another pope. In 1146, Bernard preached the second crusade before the king and queen of France and a vast assembly of knights and peasants. He then toured France and Germany promoting the crusade, apparently supporting his teaching with miracles—thirty-six in one day, it was said. But the crusade itself was a failure and a source of great disappointment to

Bernard. Although orthodox, Bernard spoke out against those who attacked Jews. He was worn out at the age of sixty-two and, although his monks prayed for his recovery, he died. He was remembered as a man of enormous power and influence, yet characterized by humility and childlike simplicity. Among his emblems are the beehive, symbolizing eloquence, and a chained dragon, symbolizing his fight against heresy. His feast day is 20 August.

Birinus [died 649]

Also known as **Berin** or **Birin**, he was probably born in Lombardy in Italy. In 633, with the approval of Pope Honorius, he sailed from Genoa to preach the Gospel in the parts of Britain it had not yet reached. By this time, Birinus had been created bishop. He landed near Southampton and started to preach to the local populace. He travelled in search of their king, and tradition has it that the Gospel was first preached on a hill near Wallingford. The king (Cynegils) was baptised soon afterwards, with Oswald, king of Northumbria, as his sponsor. The kings established Birinus at Dorchester, where he built a cathedral, but after which little is known of the remaining years of his life. He died in 649 at Dorchester, and his body was taken to Winchester when the West Saxon see was moved there. His feast day is 3 December.

Blasius [died 316]

Also called **Blaise**, St Blasius was a physician. Because of his piety and humility, he was chosen to be bishop of Sebaste in Armenia. During Diocletian's persecution, Blasius took refuge in a cave, but his hiding-place was discovered. Some accounts suggest he was betrayed, others that he healed a wild beast's wound, attracting so many wild animals to his cave that people became curious and he was found. The governor, Agricolaus, sent soldiers to arrest Blasius, and he was brought before a tribunal. Agricolaus ordered that he be beaten and, when Blasius remained obdurate, the governor had the flesh torn from his back with metal hooks. Finally, along with his two children, Blasius was beheaded. His feast day is 3 February.

Bonaventure [1221–1274]

Also called **Bonaventura**, St Bonaventure's real name was John of Fidenza. He was born in Tuscany in northern Italy and became a Franciscan monk when he was twenty-two. Ten years later saw him a teacher of theology in Paris, and in 1256 he became general of his monastic order. He governed strictly but fairly. His influence helped to reconcile differences that had arisen among cardinals on the death of Pope Clement IV in 1268 and secured the election of Gregory X. The new pope created Bonaventure bishop of Albano and cardinal in 1273, and he attended the Council of Lyons in 1274, where he died from exhaustion. He was honoured with a funeral of great pomp and splendour, attended by the pope, the king and all the cardinals. Bonaventure was one of the most eminent Catholic theologians. Because of his pure nature and the miracles that were attributed to him, he was treated with special reverence, even during his lifetime. The great Italian poet Dante placed him among the saints in his *Paradiso*. He was canonized in 1482 and in 1587 was nominated by Sixtus V as one of the great 'doctors of the church'.

In art, he may be depicted with a cardinal's hat at his feet or in a tree, holding a cross, a chalice and a book. His religious fervour earned him the title Doctor Seraphicus. Franciscans hold Bonaventure in particularly high regard. Much of his writing was devoted to praising his order, as well as to defending veneration of the Virgin Mary (Mariolatry), celibacy, transubstantiation and other doctrines and practices of the Middle Ages. He did more than any other early theologian to give scientific form to mysticism. His feast day is 15 July.

Boniface [c. 680–755]

St Boniface was born, Winfrid, at Crediton in Devon, the son of wealthy parents. It is thought he took the name Boniface when he became a monk. When he was a small child, he overheard some monks talking about their mission to the heathens in Europe, and he there and then resolved to become a monk and a missionary himself. At first, Winfrid's father opposed his decision but relented when his son was cured of a grave illness. After an education in Exeter, Winfrid joined a monastery in Hampshire, and soon became famous as a preacher. He never forgot his youthful dream of preaching to the heathens, however, and crossed the sea in 716 with Willibrord of Northumbria to convert the Frisians in that part of Europe that corresponds to modern Holland. Boniface was immediately frustrated in his purpose. The king of Frisia, Radbod, had been on the point of being converted but drew back at the font when he was told that his unbaptised ancestors were in Hell. Radbod thought he would prefer to join his ancestors than dwell in the Heavenly Kingdom. He refused to allow Boniface to preach anywhere in his realm, and the missionary returned to Hampshire. Undeterred by such an inauspicious start, Boniface travelled to Rome to obtain the pope's blessing on his missionary enterprises. In 719, the pope asked Boniface to undertake the conversion of the heathen tribes of Germany. He had no sooner made a start on this mission than news reached him that Radbod had died, and he hurried back to Frisia, joined forces with Willibrord once more and laboured there for three years—with so much success this time that Willibrord wanted to make him bishop. To avoid this fate, Boniface left Frisia and returned to Germany to devote the rest of his life to the task set him in Rome. He preached to the Hessians and baptised thousands of converts. The pope sent for Boniface and in 732 consecrated him bishop of the Germans. The territory over which he had jurisdiction expanded over the years, as he became papal legate, bishop of Mainz and finally archbishop. Boniface spent a long thirty-one years struggling to impose order, discipline and faith among Christians, and to preach the Gospel to the unconverted. He created sees, founded monasteries, and recruited a large number of missionaries from England who joined him in his work. One tradition tells that the Hessians worshipped the cult of the tree sacred to the god of thunder. Boniface cut the tree down with his own hands and built a church from the timbers. His difficulties were not only with the heathens. The bishop of Mainz had killed his father's murderer. Boniface summoned a council and had the bishop deposed. In 746, he was called upon to take that office himself, which he reluctantly did. Boniface did not visit England again. He remained to the end a student and preacher as well as a man of affairs. In 754, worn out by his cares and responsibilities, he resigned his see and returned to the dream of his youth, evangelizing the Frisians. With the bishop of Utrecht, three priests, three deacons, four monks and forty-one laymen, he set off. The missionaries were well received by the heathens, and many were converted and baptised. Boniface told them to come to him on the eve of Whitsun when they would be confirmed in the church. Instead, an armed crowd attacked Boniface and his companions and killed them. His blood-stained copy of *The Advantage of Death* by St AMBROSE was preserved for many years as a relic in the monastery of Fulda, which he had founded. An emblem of his that is found in German art is a book pierced by a sword. He may also be seen baptising the converted. His feast day is 5 June.

Brendan the Navigator [484–577]

St Brendan was born at Tralee in Ireland and studied under Jarlath of Tuam and was ordained by Bishop Erc. He is remembered mainly for his voyage in a coracle in search of 'the mysterious land far from human ken'. After seven years' fruitless wandering, he returned, but set out again with sixty companions, this time in a ship of wood instead of hides, and at length after many wanderings reached 'that paradise amid the waves of the sea', possibly the Hebrides or the Northern Isles of Orkney and Shetland, or even Iceland. Brendan founded a monastery at what is now Clonfert in County Galway and died in his ninety-fourth year. *The Navigation of St Brendan* was a very popular book in western Europe as early as the eleventh century, but the two voyages were compressed into one, and many other adventures added. In maps produced before Columbus's day, 'St Brendan's Country' is placed to the south of the island of Antilia and west of the Cape Verde Islands. His feast day is 16 May.

Brice [died 443]

Also known as **Britius**, St Brice was brought up by St MARTIN in his monastery nears Tours. According to tradition, Brice had been abandoned as a baby in his cradle on the River Loire by his father, and had been adopted by Martin. Brice was a troubled and troublesome youth, but Martin prophesied that he would one day be bishop of Tours. He was chosen to succeed Martin in that office, but his pride made him unpopular, and eventually he was accused of immoral behaviour and was driven from the see. After he had been absent for more than thirty years, the charges that had been levelled against him appeared to have been groundless. Brice ruled as bishop for the last seven years of his life. He enjoyed a great reputation for sanctity, and it is regrettable that the record of his life is all of his degenerate early years rather than his saintly old age. His feast day is 13 November.

Bride *see* **Bridgit**.

Bridgit [453–523]

Also known as **Brigid** and, in England and Scotland, as **Bride**, St Bridgit was born near Dundalk in Ulster. Her father had royal blood and, it is thought, was not legally married to her mother. Her father's legal wife was jealous and sold Bridgit's mother to a wizard who brought the girl up.

Everything that Bridgit set her hand to prospered. Under her instruction, the wizard and his wife were converted to Christianity, and she converted many heathens. When the wizard became a Christian, he gave Bridgit her freedom. He also gave Bridgit's mother her freedom, and they both returned to Bridgit's father. But because Bridgit was inclined to give her father's cattle and goods to the poor, he determined to sell her into slavery again. He offered her to the king of Leinster, who refused on the grounds that 'her merit is higher before God than before men'. Bridgit's father then tried to marry her off, but she refused. Finally, with her father's consent, she was dedicated to Christ by Bishop Mel. Her most notable achievement after this was the foundation of the Abbey of Kildare, a monastery for both men and women. She chose a hermit to be her bishop. Many miracles are attributed to Bridgit. In one, she restored the sight of a blind nun who could not share Bridgit's pleasure in the beauty of the sunset. (The nun then asked Bridgit to take her sight away again for 'when the world is so visible to the eyes, God is less clear to the soul'.) Bridgit died at Kildare on 1 February and was buried there. For centuries after her death, the nuns of her community kept a fire burning constantly at her tomb to honour her memory. Her feast day is 1 February.

Bruno [c. 1040–1101]
Bruno was born at Cologne and received his earliest education there. Subsequently he became rector of the cathedral school at Rheims in France, but, depressed by the wickedness of his times, in 1086, with six companions, he went to the wild mountain country of Chartreuse, near Grenoble,

where he founded the order of the Carthusians, one of the most austere of the monastic orders. Bruno and his companions each had a seperate cell in which they practised the severities of the rule of St BENEDICT, keeping silence during six days of the week and seeing one another only on Sundays. Pope Urban II, who had been one of Bruno's most eminent scholars, summoned him to Rome in 1089. Bruno obeyed the call reluctantly and steadily refused all offers of preferment. In 1094 he established a second Carthusian monastery at Della Torre, in a solitary district of Calabria, where he died. He left no written regulations for his followers, these first appearing in a complete form in 1581. He was canonized in 1628. His feast day is 6 October.

Brigid *see* **Bridgit**.

Britius *see* **Brice**.

C

Catherine of Alexandria [fourth century]

Very little is known that is certain about the life of St Catherine, although many stories and legends grew up around her name. It is said she was a native of Alexandria and was young, beautiful, very rich and learned. She attracted the attention of the emperor, Maximian. When Catherine refused his advances, the emperor confronted her with an assembly of the most learned heathen philosophers in an attempt to overcome her scruples. She argued for the truth of Christian teaching and defeated the philosophers completely. In a rage, Maximian ordered that she be broken on a wheel studded with spikes. Catherine survived this torture, but was then scourged and beheaded. In art, she can be represented alongside the spiked wheel or with the sword with which she was beheaded. Her body was said to have been taken by angels and buried on Mount Sinai. For centuries, Catherine was the most popular saint in the calendar. The crusaders brought her fame to England, where she was as much venerated as she was on the continent. Her feast day became a popular holiday, and no fewer than eighty churches were dedicated in her honour, as well as many chapels and wayside shrines. Her feast day is 25 November.

Catherine of Siena [1348–1380]

St Catherine was one of twenty-five children born to a prosperous dyer in Siena. As a child, she was very religious and when she was six, had a vision of Christ. Her parents wanted Catherine to marry, but she was determined to join an order of sisters called the Mantellatae who, although bound by vows, lived at home rather than in a religious community. Catherine fasted frequently and led a life of extreme mortification, spending much time in prayer and contemplation. At one time she was greatly troubled by impure thoughts and images, but soon afterwards she saw Jesus on the Cross and he spoke to her. On the strength of his words, Catherine lived as a recluse in a single room. But after three years, an inner voice told her that she must go into the world, which she did and devoted herself to tending the sick and other good works. She was indefatigable during a time of plague and worked many miracles of healing. During the plague of 1374, she heard that the director of the hospital had contracted the disease and that his condition was critical. Catherine walked into his sick room and addressed him cheerfully, upon which he ate a meal, got up and was cured. At first many people were jealous of Catherine and slanderous stories were spread about her. She was unmoved by these expressions of ingratitude. At about this time, she is said to have had a vision of Christ holding a crown of gold in one hand and a crown of thorns in the other. He asked her which she would choose and, without hesitating, she chose the crown of thorns. Although busily occupied in the world, Catherine was a mystic. She continued to spend many hours in prayer and contemplation and was sometimes lost in a state of ecstasy. Impressive as her cures of the body were, she was even more successful with the soul. Sinners of every kind, apparently impervious to all other influences, yielded to her. Few could resist in her presence. Once, two worldly friars tried to shame her by asking difficult theological questions. She answered discreetly and modestly and accused them of seeking not truth but praise and glory in the eyes of men. From that moment, the lives of these men were changed. Catherine was also known as a peacemaker and was often called on to mediate in trade disputes, domestic quarrels and family feuds. Her influence spread far beyond Siena and much of her correspondence survives. Pope Gregory XI, then at Avignon, used her as his intermediary and, in return, she did not hesitate to give the pope the benefit of her advice. She visited him in Avignon with the purpose of persuading him to return to Rome. The cardinals were against her, and Gregory feared assassination. But Catherine prevailed. Then, as her life was at risk, she went to Florence, which was engaged in a civil war. She succeeded in bringing peace and reconciling the city to the pope. Towards the end of her life, Catherine attempted to promote the cause of Pope Urban VI and to recall him to better ways. She was pious to the end and was praying when she died. Among her emblems in art are the cross, the lily (the symbol of purity), a book (in allusion to her writings), the rosary, and the marks of the stigmata. Her feast day is 29 April.

Cecilia [third century]

There are no historical accounts of St Cecilia. It is said that she was married to a man called Valerian, but prayed daily that she might preserve her virginity. She told her husband that she was under the protection of an angel. When he asked to see this angel, Cecilia told him that if he believed in God and would be baptised, he would see the angel. Valerian consented and was baptised by the pope. On returning from his baptism, he saw his wife kneeling with, by her side, an angel with outstretched wings and holding two crowns of roses and lilies. These Valerian placed on the women's heads and vanished. Soon afterwards, Cecilia was condemned for her Christianity and was put to death by suffocation in the baths. St Cecilia's church in Rome is built on the site of the bath in which she died. Later, Cecilia was taken to be patron saint of music, and she is generally represented artistically with an organ or organ-pipes, or conversely, shown surrounded by broken musical instruments—a rejection of earthly for heavenly music. This may be because Pope Paschal I, who translated her relics with great pomp in 817, endowed the monks of the monastery next to the church of St Cecilia, where her bones lay, so that they might sing at her tomb all day and all night. Her feast day is 22 November.

Cedd [died 664]

St Cedd was the brother of St CHAD. A Northumbrian, he was one of the four priests sent by Bishop Finan, at the request of the newly baptised King Paeda, to instruct and baptise the Mercians. But Cedd's most important work was to be done among the East Saxons, who had relapsed into heathendom after their conversion by Mellitus. Cedd was so successful that Finan consecrated him bishop of the East Saxons. So great was Cedd's moral force that the East Saxon king knelt and begged for pardon after he had visited the home of an excommunicant. He visited his homeland often and founded the Abbey of Lastingham. On his last visit there, he fell sick and died. Thirty of his monks resolved to live near his body or to die. It is said that all, except one young boy, died. His feast day is 7 January.

Celestine V [1215–1296]

Born in Naples as Peter di Morrone, he devoted himself to a life of ascetic severities and founded the order of the Celestines. Much against his will, he was elected pope in 1294, when he was nearly eighty years old. After only five months he resigned his office (known as 'the great refusal') which led the great Italian poet Dante to place him at the entrance to Hell in his *Divine Comedy*. Celestine was imprisoned by his successor, Boniface VIII. He was canonized in 1313. His feast day until 1969 was 19 May.

Chad [died 672]

St Chad was one of four brothers who were all priests. He was a monk at the Abbey of Lastingham and succeeded his brother St CEDD as abbot. King Oswy sent Chad to be bishop of York in place of WILFRID, who had delayed his return from France. Chad immediately devoted himself to the duties of his office, and studied and preached in towns and villages. When Theodore of Tarsus became archbishop, he challenged Chad's consecration. Although the fault was put right, Theodore decided that Wilfrid was the rightful bishop, and Chad withdrew to Lastingham. He was brought out of retirement to be bishop of the Mercians. His seat was at Lichfield where he governed for more than two years. His humility was such that he always journeyed on foot, until Theodore ordered him onto a horse and put him onto it with his own hands. Chad built a small oratory near his church, where he prayed and read with some of the brethren. He was warned of his approaching death by an angel. He died on 2 March and was buried by St Mary's Church. His body was later moved to the church of St Peter and to the present cathedral at Lichfield in 1148. His feast day is 2 March.

Charles I [1600–1649]

King Charles I is the only saint canonized by the English church since the Reformation. It has been said that, had he been willing to give up episcopacy and consent to the destruction of the Church of England, he could have saved his throne and his life. Charles was an affectionate father and a faithful and loving husband—virtues not commonly found among kings. He was devout and punctilious in the performance of religious duties. He never failed to have part of the Liturgy read to him before he sat down to dinner. Like all men, he sinned, but he repented sincerely of his sins. Although his political views are now discredited, he was an honourable man who loved his country. After he had been executed, he was buried in St George's Chapel at Windsor. Miracles have been attributed to him. Charles was formally canonized by the Church of England after the Restoration, and was known as King Charles the Martyr. A form of service was drawn up, but was withdrawn by royal warrant in 1859. Five churches were built and dedicated to him in the seventeenth century. His feast day is 30 January.

Charles Borromeo [1538–1584]

Born to a noble family at Arona on Lake Maggiore in northern Italy, he studied law at Pavia and took the degree of doctor in 1559. The next year his uncle, Pope Puis IV, appointed him in quick succession apostolic protonotary, cardinal and archbishop of Milan. As a counsellor of the pope, the young cardinal showed wisdom beyond his years, did much to bring the Council of Trent to a successful conclusion, and had the principal part in drawing up the *Catechismus Romanus*. The simplicity of his manners, his piety, and his devotion to duty, made him an ideal bishop, but his severe morality and determined efforts to maintain ecclesiastical disipline made him enemies, and in 1569 he was even shot at as he knelt at prayer in his chapel. He devoted the greater part of his revenues to the relief of the poor, and during a famine in 1570, and the plague at Milan in 1576, he showed much energetic benevolence and fearless devotion. He founded in 1570 the Helvetic College at Milan to provide priests for Switzerland and brought about an alliance of the seven Catholic cantons. He was canonized in 1610. His emblems include a crucifix and skull. He is sometimes depicted wearing the rope of the penitent around his neck. His feast day is 4 November.

Christopher [third century?]

There is more than one version of the life of St Christopher. The most common account in the west tells us that he was a man of stature who wanted to serve the most powerful master. He turned to Christ after a king and the Devil had both proved inadequate. As he carried a child across a river, his burden suddenly became almost too heavy for him and its voice revealed that he was in fact carrying Christ. (In Greek, the name Christophoros means 'the one who carries Christ'.) Christopher was martyred during the Decian persecution because of his Christian faith. In the Middle Ages, it was believed that those who had seen a representation of St Christopher would come to no harm, and he came to be the patron saint of travellers. In more modern times, he is the patron saint of motorists. His emblem is the staff that Christ transformed into a palm tree bearing dates. His feast day is 25 July.

Clare [*c.* 1194–1253]

St Clare was born into a noble family in Assisi in Italy. When she was eighteen, and when she had already turned down more than one offer of marriage, she left home and joined the Benedictine nuns at Bastia. She had come under the influence of ST FRANCIS OF ASSISI. She was joined at this convent by her sister and her widowed mother. These three women founded the order of Poor Ladies, which were called Minoresses in England and are now known as the Poor Clares. Pope Innocent III granted Clare the privilege that she and her sisters might live on alms and would not require to own any worldly goods. Over the years, attempts were made to modify the rules under which the nuns lived, but Clare fought to preserve the way of life laid down for them by St Francis. St Clare ruled her community for forty years, despite enjoying indifferent health. In the Middle Ages, she was much revered for her contemplative life. She is the patron saint of television. Her emblems include a monstrance, a lily, or a cross and a crozier. Her feast day is 11 August.

Clement I [died *c*. 100]

St Clement is said to have been the third bishop of Rome after the Apostles. He was certainly among the first and is said to have been ordained by St PETER. He wrote the first Epistle of Clement to the Corinthians, a letter of great historical importance because of the evidence it contains on the apostolic appointment of the clergy at Corinth during his time. It is probable that he is not the Clement mentioned by St PAUL in his Epistle to the Philippians, although he may be identified with the consul, Flavius Clemens, who is recorded as having been put to death by the emperor, Domitian. He is often depicted being accompanied by a lamb and leaning on an anchor or with an anchor around his neck. His feast day is 23 November.

Colman of Lindisfarne [died 676]

St Colman was an Irishman, who became a monk at Iona and was sent to Lindisfarne to preach to the English. He became bishop of Lindisfarne in 661 and immediately became embroiled in the controversy about the date of Easter. At the Synod of Whitby, which met to decide the issue, Colman promoted the Celtic position against WILFRID, advocating the Catholic view. Colman claimed to follow the teaching of St JOHN THE EVANGELIST and COLUMBA while Wilfrid took his inspiration from St PETER and the rest of the Catholic church. The king of Northumbria, Oswy, decided in Wilfrid's favour, and Colman returned to Ireland, taking with him those monks who would not accept the ruling. He also took some of the bones of St AIDAN, leaving the rest in the church at Lindisfarne. Colman and the monastery over which he ruled had cattle but no money. Any money that they were given they in turn gave to the poor. They felt no need for a lavish lifestyle, even for entertaining grand visitors. The king himself came with only five or six servants, and left when he had performed his devotions. They ate simply, and their only care was to serve God, not the world, and to feed the soul, not the body. The priests went into the villages to preach and baptise, and to visit the sick. When he left Lindisfarne, Colman first went to Iona, where he stayed for four years. Then he retired to the island of Inishbofin, off the coast of Mayo. Here, he built his monastery. There was some dissension between the Irish and the English monks, principally regarding the division of labour and the taking in of the harvest. So Colman built another monastery in Mayo for the English monks. He himself lived with the Irish brethren on Inishbofin, where he died on 8 August. His feast day is 18 February (and 8 August in the Irish calendar).

Columba [*c.* 521–597]

St Columba was born in Ireland, probably in Donegal, into the O'Donnell clan. His father and mother both had royal blood. He was called Colum, which means 'dove'. Little is known about his early life, but history records that he became a monk and, while still a young man, started to found monasteries, the first of them at Derry and the most famous at Kells. His favourite pastime was copying manuscripts, and he is said to have transcribed three hundred copies of the Gospels with his own hand. He quarrelled with King Diarmid and called on his kinsmen to exact vengeance. Many were killed in the ensuing battle, and Columba was condemned by a synod and excommunicated. Later, the sentence was withdrawn and Columba was instructed to win to Christ as many heathen souls as Christians had perished in the battle. He was not satisfied by this outcome and sought the counsel of a hermit, only to have the synod's ruling confirmed, and that he was to suffer permanent exile from Ireland. Columba resolved to go, and twelve of his followers elected to go with him. At the age of forty-two, he set out in a coracle. He first landed on the island of Oronsay, but turned away as he could still see Ireland from it. He then settled on Iona, a barren island off the west coast of Scotland, where he built a chapel. For about two years, Columba ministered to the Irish settlers in the neighbourhood, who were already converted to Christianity. Then he turned his attention to preaching to the heathen Picts in various parts of Scotland. His time was divided between journeying in the central belt of Scotland—where he met Druids, built churches, and founded monasteries—and sojourns in Iona, where he prayed, studied, copied the Gospels, worked manually with the monks and received the many visitors who were drawn to the island by Columba's fame. All types of people came— peasants whose crops had failed, women who had quarrelled with their husbands, and at least four men who had themselves founded monasteries. Columba was 'confessor' to two kings and a saint as well as to a host of lesser men and women. Those who came found him sympathetic and helpful. He particularly loved to bless young children, and even cattle. He is believed to have had the gift of second sight. He had a vision in which King Aidan joined battle with the barbarians, and Columba called upon the monks to pray. Aidan

was victorious, and several days later news reached
Columba that what he had 'seen' had indeed happened. A biography of Columba was written by St ADAMNAN, in which
his last days are recorded. On the day he died, according to
Adamnan, Columba blessed the granary and climbed the little hill to bless the monastery. He then returned to his cell
and copied the Thirty-fourth Psalm. He spent the night in his
cell on his bed of bare rock, with a stone for a pillow, and
gave his last commands to his disciples. He urged them to be
charitable and to pursue peace. When the chapel bell rang, he
rose and hastened to the chapel and knelt before the altar.
They found him lying there and, although he could no longer
speak, he lifted his hands to bless them, and died. His feast
day is 9 June.

Columban [543–615]

St Columban was one of the most learned and eloquent of the
many missionaries sent from Ireland to the continent of Europe during the Dark Ages. He was born in Leinster and
studied under St Comgall, abbot of the monastery of Bangor
on the coast of Down. When he was forty, he went to France
with twelve companions and founded monasteries at
Anegray, Luxeuil and Fontaines. His adherence to the Irish
rule for calculating the date of Easter brought him into conflict with the French bishops in 602, and the courage with
which he rebuked the vices of the Burgundian court led to his
expulsion. After a number of journeys and adventures,
Columban settled at Bregenz, near Lake Constance. After a
year or two, he moved on to Lombardy, and in 612 founded
the monastery of Bobbio in the Apennines. He died there on

21 November. A biography of Columban was written by Jonas, abbot of Bobbio. Columban's own writings, all in Latin, comprise a rule for the government of his monastery, six poems on the vanity of life, several letters on ecclesiastical affairs, seventeen short sermons and a commentary on the Psalms. The town of San Colombano, near Milan, is named after him. His emblem is a bear. His feast days are 21 and 23 November.

Crispin and Crispinian [died 285]

St Crispin and his brother Crispinian are commemorated together in the Roman calendar. They were born in Rome and worked as shoemakers in Soissons, a city in northern France that has Roman remains. During a local persecution, they were denounced as Christians and beheaded. The brothers are patron saints of shoemakers. Their names were made famous by William Shakespeare in his play *Henry V*, in which the battle of Agincourt is fought on St Crispin's day. Their feast day is 25 October.

Cuthbert [died 687]

St Cuthbert is thought to have been born the son of poor parents in Lothian in Scotland. His childhood home was near the monastery of Tiningham. Cuthbert was a lively and energetic boy. In 651, he was tending sheep on the banks of the River Lauder when he saw, in a vision, the soul of St AIDAN transported to heaven. Next morning, he resolved to become a monk. He went to the monastery of Melrose and presented himself to the prior. He was greeted with the words, 'Behold, a servant of the Lord'. In the monastery Cuthbert surpassed the other monks in the strictness with which he observed the rules of the order, in his studying, labours and prayer. He took no intoxicating drink. After a few years, Cuthbert moved to a new monastery at Ripon where he was appointed to look after guests. But in 661, Cuthbert and those monks who would not forsake their Celtic observances for those of Rome, were expelled and returned to Melrose. Cuthbert became prior. He often went out of the monastery and preached in the local villages. He was noted for venturing into areas that others hesitated to visit, sometimes staying away for as long as a month. Like many saints, Cuthbert attracted wild animals. One night, he was praying by the sea when two otters came out of the water to play at his feet. When they had received his blessing, they returned to the sea. On another occasion, when Cuthbert and a companion were far from human habitation and had no food, they saw an eagle settle by a river and there they found a large fish, freshly caught. Cuthbert divided the fish in half, instructed his companion to return one half to the bird, and they made a meal of the other half. Cuthbert was later made prior of Lindisfarne with a brief to introduce Roman observances, to which he had become reconciled. His patience and even temper helped him overcome the resistance that he inevitably encountered. He prayed with such devotion that it was not unknown for him to spend three or four nights at prayer. In 676, when he had been at Lindisfarne for twelve years, Cuthbert obtained the abbot's permission to retire to one of the Farne islands to seek greater solitude. His island is now known as House Island. With the help of the brothers there, he built himself a cell and an oratory, and surrounded them with a wall so high that he could see only the sky. At first, when the brethren visited Cuthbert, he used to wash their feet. But gradually he seems to have had contact only with a few who came to consult him about their spiritual health. He cultivated a barren patch of land on which to grow food to support himself. He used to preach to the birds to keep them off his barley. In 685, Cuthbert was elected bishop of Lindisfarne, an office that he accepted with the greatest reluctance and only after the king and many others had visited him on his island and urged him to accept. He ruled as bishop for two years. Two months after Christmas in 687, Cuthbert fell ill and died. He was buried on Lindisfarne but, when the Viking raids began, his remains were moved to Durham. His feast day is 20 March.

Cyprian [died 258]

St Cyprian was a leading member of the legal fraternity in Carthage. He was renowned for his erudition, eloquence and gracious manner. He was already into middle age when he was converted and baptised. He had thought it would be too difficult to shake off his old life and adopt a new one, but his baptism appeared to banish any doubts. He sold his estates and gave the proceeds to the poor, but his gardens were bought by his friends and given back to him. Cyprian studied Christian literature eagerly. Soon after his baptism, he was ordained a priest and when, in 248, the bishop of Carthage died, Cyprian was chosen by popular acclaim as his successor. Soon after Cyprian's accession, the Decian persecution began and threw the church in Africa into confusion. Many fled; many were martyred. Cyprian himself left Carthage, for which he was attacked, although he successfully defended his actions. The church needed someone to direct, advise and encourage, and it was better that such a person should not be in the direct line of fire. After fifteen months, in 251, Cyprian returned to Carthage. The persecution was not yet over, and he soon faced new troubles. He had to make a decision about those who had lapsed during the persecution and now wished to return to the church. Some confessors claimed to have the authority to release from all penalties those to whom they gave letters of peace. Cyprian refused to allow this claim and insisted that apostates must be judged on their individual merits. He called a synod of African bishops, which formulated a number of decrees on how the lapsed were to be treated. Cyprian's aim was to avoid the extremes of undue harshness or excessive leniency. A schism was created by those who favoured the lenient approach, but Cyprian successfully procured condemnation of these at the synod. Prompted by the schism, he wrote a treatise, *On Unity*. His thesis was that the episcopate was founded to be the focus of unity, and he worked out the idea of episcopal succession from the Apostles. He condemned those who simply assumed the title of bishop without authority. Peace was restored to the church in 253, but in the same year a plague broke out in Carthage. The streets were littered with the dead and dying, and the living were filled with terror. Cyprian urged all Christians to devote themselves to caring for the sick, whether Christian or pagan. Four years later, another persecution began, and Cyprian was banished. He stayed away for a year, after which an edict ordered the execution of all bishops, priests and deacons. Cyprian made no attempt to hide, and he was arrested and taken to Carthage. A large crowd, of both Christians and pagans, gathered round the house where he was being held. Next day, he was brought before the proconsul and was condemned to die by the sword. The crowd shouted that they wished to die with Cyprian. Followed by an enormous crowd and guarded by soldiers, he was taken to the place of execution. He knelt and prayed. The executioner was so nervous that he could not perform his task, and it was left to a centurion to sever Cyprian's neck. All day, crowds came to view his body; at night it was taken by Christians for burial. His feast day is 16 September.

Cyril [827–869] and Methodius [826–885]

Cyril and Methodius were brothers and natives of Thessalonica, Cyril changing his name from Constantine when he became a monk. Cyril had been a disciple of Photius, and because of his learning was surnamed 'the philosopher.' About 860, the Khazars, a Tartar people who inhabited the country from the northeast of the Black Sea to the lower Volga, asked for Christian missionaries. Cyril was sent in answer to their appeal and made many converts. Methodius evangelized the Bulgarians of Thrace and Moesia and baptised their king, Bogoris, in 861. The brothers prepared Slav translations of the Scriptures and the main liturgical books (which became the foundation of Slav literature) and became known as the Apostles of the Slavs, thus antagonizing German Catholic missionaries in the Slav countries. The two brothers were summoned to Rome to explain their conduct, and Cyril died there in 869. Methodius, who in the same year was consecrated bishop of the Moravians in Rome, completed the evangelization of the Slavs. Called to Rome a second time in 879 to justify his celebration of the Mass in the vernacular, he succeeded in gaining the approval of Pope John VIII. He returned to his diocese in 880. Both brothers are recognized as saints by the Roman Catholic Church after having been condemned as Arians by several popes (including GREGORY VII). The Cyrillic alphabet, modified from Greek by Cyril, superseded the more ancient Slavonic alphabet over a wide area. Their feast day is 14 February (11 May in the Greek Church).

Cyril of Alexandria [376–444]

Cyril was born in Alexandria and brought up by his uncle, Theophilus, patriarch of the city. After some years as a monk in the Nitrian desert, Cyril succeeded his uncle as patriarch in 412. He proceded to close the churches of the Novatians, and in 415 expelled the Jews from the city. The latter part of his life was devoted to relentless persecution of the Syrian priest Nestorius for his refusal to apply to the Virgin Mary the epithet *Theotokos* ('Mother of God'). The ecumenical council of Ephesus in 431 condemned Nestorius for his doctrine of the two natures of Christ. A number of bishops led by John of Antioch, who had arrived at Ephesus too late to take part in the discussion, convened a synod of their own and condemned Cyril. The emperor confirmed both these depositions, but Cyril, notwithstanding, kept his patriarchate until his death. His feast day is 27 June.

Cyril of Jerusalem [315–386]

St Cyril was bishop of Jerusalem from 350 until his death. He lived at a time when the Arians, who denied Christ's divinity, were dominant in the church, and throughout his long episcopate he was persecuted and harassed by them. In 358 he was condemned by a council of Arian bishops for selling ornaments belonging to the church to buy food for the poor, and he was expelled from Jerusalem. Cyril was restored by one council, then condemned by another. Recalled for a second time by the emperor, Julian, on his accession, Cyril prophesied correctly that Julian would be thwarted in his attempt to rebuild the temple of Jerusalem. Eighteen lectures of Cyril's have survived—originally delivered on evenings in Lent in the basilica of the Holy Cross in Jerusalem. They constitute an early formal system of theology, and are a valuable source of evidence of the church's teaching at that time on the creed, the sacraments and ritual. His feast day is 18 March.

D

Damasus I [*c*. 306–384]

Probably born in Rome and possibly of Spanish descent, Damasus became archdeacon of the Roman Church in 355 and pope in 366. His election as pope was violently contested, resulting in a bloody three-day struggle in the streets of Rome. The Emperor Valentinian I decided in favour of Damasus, and twelve years later, the schism still continuing, an edict of Gratian in 378 made him the judge in the cases concerning all the clergy of the hostile party who still lived in Rome. He was a zealous opponent of the Arians and condemned the Illyrian bishops Ursacius and Valens at a synod that he held at Rome in 368, and Auxentius, bishop of Milan, at a second synod there in 370. Damasus induced his friend and secretary JEROME to undertake the Vulgate. His feast day is 11 December.

David [died *c*. 601]

Also known as **Dewi**, St David is the patron saint of Wales. Very little is known about his life. He presided at two synods of the Welsh church and was an apostle to the Welsh people. He founded many monasteries in south Wales. He is said to have made a pilgrimage to Jerusalem and to have been consecrated archbishop, but there is no historical evidence for this. It is also said that a synod of Welsh bishops met and condemned the Pelagian heresy (Pelagius denied man's need of divine grace) and then endeavoured to promulgate its decrees among a vast crowd that had gathered to hear them. The bishops looked with dismay at the thousands of people. None could make himself heard. David was sent for. Reluctantly he came and stood on the flat ground. As he preached, the ground rose under his feet and became a mountain, and on the top of the mountain a church was set. As a result, David is said to have been made archbishop of Menevia (the modern St Davids), although it is doubtful whether he ever received metropolitan authority from Rome. He kept in close touch with Irish bishops—his seat was easily accessible from Ireland—and he was a good and faithful bishop, building many churches and teaching diligently. David died on 1 March, possibly in 601, although the year is uncertain. A vast crowd gathered to receive his last blessing and were overcome with grief when he died. His emblem is a leek. His feast day is 1 March.

Denis [died 273]

Also known as **Denys** or **Dionysius**, but not to be confused with Dionysius, the friend and companion of St PAUL, St Denis is the patron saint of France. He was sent by CLEMENT to preach the Gospel in Gaul (modern France), eventually settling in Paris. The inhabitants of the city did not receive him kindly, and he was put to death at Montmartre, which means 'martyr's mount'. According to one account, his body rose up after the execution, took its head under its arm and, attended by an angel, walked with it to the site of the abbey

of St Denys. Denis is usually represented as a bishop holding
his head in his hands. His feast day is 9 October.

Dionysius (of Paris) *see* **Denis**.

Dominic [1170–1221]
St Dominic was a Spaniard, from Castile, and the founder of
the famous order of friar-preachers. He was born Domingo
de Guzman. Like St FRANCIS OF ASSISI, he inaugurated a new
kind of monastic life. Previously, the prevailing policy had
been of separation from the world, to join Christ and to pray
for the salvation of the world. The monks of St Francis and
St Dominic were to renounce the world but to save it, not by
leaving it but by being part of it and by engaging in missionary activity. Dominic was educated at the university of
Palencia. It is said that he sold his clothes and books to provide for the poor during a famine and, on one occasion, to
have been ready to sell himself into slavery to redeem a man
taken captive by the Moors. He was made canon of Osma
when he was twenty-five, and was renowned for the length
and earnestness of his prayers. He is said to have spent whole
nights in the church in prayer. The idea for his preaching order came to him during a visit to Languedoc in 1206. He
found that weapons of persecution rather than preaching
were used to convert heretics (Languedoc was the centre of
Albigensian heresy). Dominic combated the heresy by giving clear and simple teaching on the Incarnation and by de-
vising simple devotions for people who were unable to use
prayer manuals. In 1215, he obtained Pope Innocent III's
permission to establish his order of preachers. The preachers

were to be independent of the bishops, an innovation that Innocent is said to have hesitated over—hitherto, bishops had been responsible for providing preaching in their dioceses. Dominic's order spread rapidly, and within five years there were Dominican converts in Italy, Spain, France, Germany and Poland. In 1221, Dominic fell sick in Venice. Knowing that he was dying, he insisted on being taken to a monastery belonging to his order at Bologna, wnere he died on 6 August. He was a humble and devout man, even if his name sometimes suggests sternness to some. He is often depicted holding a lily or a book, with a star on or above his forehead, sometimes accompanied by a black and white dog with a torch in its mouth (possibly a pun on his name 'Domini canis'). His feast day is 8 August.

Dunstan [*c.* 924–988]

St Dunstan was the son of a West Saxon nobleman who had royal blood. The family estates were near Glastonbury, and Dunstan was educated at the abbey there. At the court of Athelstan, king of Wessex and Mercia, Dunstan is said to have had dreams and visions that he believed to be supernatural. He was a studious boy, unpopular with his peers. They complained about Dunstan to the king and accused him of practising magic. Dunstan was banished from the court, and his critics are said to have bound his hands and feet and thrown him into a marsh. Dunstan went to ALPHEGE, to whom he was related and who was bishop of Winchester. Alphege tried to persuade Dunstan to become a monk. At first Dunstan refused on the grounds that he might one day wish to marry, but when he recovered from a serious illness, he

changed his mind, took his vows and went to live at Glastonbury. There he lived in a small cell and led a life of great devotion. He became a skilled worker in metal. A legend tells
that, when the Devil appeared to him in the form of a beautiful girl, Dunstan seized his nose in his blacksmith's tongs.
When EDMUND became king, Dunstan was recalled to court.
However, he was soon driven away again. One day, the king
was out hunting and became separated from his companions.
When the stag and the hounds disappeared over a cliff, it
seemed certain that the king's horse would follow. The king
uttered a prayer, and the horse stopped just in time. After his
miraculous escape, the king sent for Dunstan, and they rode
together to Glastonbury, where they knelt in prayer. The king
then installed Dunstan as abbot. Dunstan, who was still only
twenty-one, introduced stricter rules of discipline. He devoted himself to teaching, and Glastonbury became famous
as a seat of learning. Edred succeeded Edmund the following
year and offered Dunstan the bishopric of Crediton, an offer
that was refused. Dunstan fell foul of Edwy who succeeded
Edred. At his coronation feast, Edwy left the bishops to be
with a beautiful girl whom he wanted to marry but to whom
he was closely related. Dunstan was sent to bring him back.
This mission was successful, but Dunstan was soon dismissed from court and outlawed. He took refuge in Flanders,
staying in a Benedictine monastery and seeing that order's
rule in its fullest form for the first time. When the kingdom
north of the Thames revolted and made Edgar king, Dunstan
returned to his homeland and was made bishop of Worcester,
then of London. In 961, he became archbishop of Canterbury. He was the king's principal adviser and deserves much

credit for the prosperity of Edgar's reign until the king's death in 975. Dunstan devoted a lot of his energy to trying to impose order and to enforce canons that regulated the lives of the clergy. He even rebuked the king for having sinned with a nun and imposed a seven years' penance on him. Dunstan encouraged education, and every priest was required to learn a craft in order to be able to teach it to others. He was a noted peacemaker, patching up quarrels, and he befriended the poor and the needy. He celebrated for the last time on Ascension Day in 988 when he announced his approaching death. He died a few days later.His feast day is 19 May.

E

Ealdhelm *see* Aldhelm.

Edmund [841–870]
St Edmund is said to have been a Saxon prince, appointed by Offa, king of the East Anglians, to be his successor. He set sail from Kent and was shipwrecked off the coast of Norfolk at a place still known as St Edmund's Point. He was not immediately acknowledged as king and is said to have spent a year learning the Psalter by heart. A threatened Danish invasion forced the East Anglian nobles to act, and Edmund was proclaimed king. He led an army against the Danes but was defeated. After the battle, he was summoned by the Danish victors on condition that he halve his treasure with them and become a vassal prince. Edmund was willing to split his treasure, but he refused the second condition absolutely unless his overlord became a Christian. He believed that he had been called by God to help his people lead Christian lives, a task that would be impossible as a vassal prince to a heathen Dane. The Danish prince, Hingmar, was enraged by Edmund's position and ordered him to be scourged and tied to a tree as a living target for practising Danish archers. When Edmund was killed, his body was thrown into some trees and, according to tradition, was later miraculously re-

covered with the guidance of a grey wolf. A small chapel was built on the place where his body was found. His body was later taken to the new monastery of St Edmund's Bury. His feast day is 20 November.

Edmund Rich [c. 1170–1240]

Also called **Edmund of Abingdon**, St Edmund Rich was born at Abingdon, the son of devout Christian parents. His father died when Edmund was still young, and his mother trained him carefully in religion. He studied in Paris, then taught in Oxford for several years. He returned to Paris to study theology and became a famous teacher. He was ordained into the priesthood and led a life of extreme mortification. He ate only one meal a day and slept on the bare floor. He wore a hair shirt next to his skin, and spent much time in prayer. Edmund trained many people in devotion and wrote a treatise, *Speculum Ecclesiae*. He returned to England in about 1222 and became treasurer of Salisbury Cathedral. He became famous for devotion and good works, and as a preacher. He preached a crusade at Oxford and elsewhere. In 1233, he was elected archbishop of Canterbury after three previous elections had been quashed by the pope. As archbishop, he offered a steady, if ineffectual, resistance to the rule of Henry III. A week after his consecration, he threatened to excommunicate Henry if he would not amend his government, and in 1237, he supported a move by the council to have the king's foreign advisers dismissed. Edmund also resisted the pope's attempt to tax the clergy, but ultimately without success. Eventually, he gave up in despair and retired to Pontigny, where he devoted himself to prayer.

He died at Soissy and was buried at Pontigny, where his body remains on a shrine behind the high altar. Despite Henry III's resistance, Edmund was canonized in 1247. His feast day is 16 November.

Edward the Confessor [c. 1004–1066]

St Edward the Confessor was the son of Ethelred the Unready and Emma of Normandy. He was educated at the monastery school at Ely, then was sent to Normandy where he lived until becoming king in 1042. He appears not to have been a strong king. Although devoted to hunting, he took more interest in the cloister than in affairs of state. However, after the Norman conquest in 1066, the English tended to look nostalgically at Edward's reign as something of a golden age. He was devout, restrained in his appetites and charitable. In a rough and brutal age, Edward was conspicuous by his devotion, gentleness and goodness. He was also something of an idealist and tried to live up to his ideals. He was called 'Confessor', not because he was constantly confessing his sins, but because he had suffered for his faith by having to go into exile for fear of the heathen Danes. Edward's greatest work was the building of Westminster Abbey, which was dedicated a few days before he died. It was by far the most magnificent building in the land and brought distinction to this king's reign. Edward is said to have worked many miracles both before and after he came to the throne. His feast day is 13 October.

Edward the Martyr [c. 963–978]

Edward the Martyr was brought up by the bishop of Crediton

and succeeded his father as king of the West Saxons when he
was only twelve years old. When he went to visit his stepbrother Ethelred at Corfe, he was given a cup of wine and
was stabbed in the back. His body was buried without honour in unconsecrated ground, but two years later, it was taken
with great ceremony by DUNSTAN and buried at Shaftesbury.
Many miracles were said to have taken place at his tomb. It
is not entirely clear why Edward was canonized, although it
may have been because of his stepbrother's feelings of guilt
and an outburst of popular feeling. His feast day is 18 March.

Elizabeth of Hungary [1205–1229]

St Elizabeth was a Hungarian princess. While still a young
child, she was betrothed to the eldest son of the Landgrave of
Thuringia and was sent to be brought up with him at
Wartburg. She married him when she was fifteen. Before her
marriage, she went in state to the Church of Our Lady at
Eisenach, took off her coronet, and threw herself on her
knees before a large crucifix. She was rebuked for this act,
but said that she could not pass before Christ with jewels on
her head. After marriage, Elizabeth spent all her spare time
helping the poor and nursing the sick. She prayed every day,
and often arose during the night to attend to her devotions.
She gave tools instead of money to the needy and took crip-
pled children into her house. She even allowed a leper child
to lie in her husband's bed when he was away. He returned
and, furious at finding the leper there, tore off the bedclothes
to find the form of the Infant Jesus lying there. Elizabeth did
all she could to relieve distress during a famine. In 1227,
Elizabeth's husband went on a crusade and was dead within

a few months. Her brother-in-law drove Elizabeth and her children out of the castle at Wartburg, and she suffered every kind of hardship without complaining. Eventually, she settled at Marburg and, living a life of the greatest simplicity, she devoted herself to caring for the sick in a hospital she built with what little money she had left. She sold her clothes and her jewellery and spun wool to meet immediate expenses. She washed the sores of lepers. She was bright and cheerful and lit up the lives of everyone who came near her. Worn out by work and troubles, Elizabeth died when she was still only twenty-four. Emblems found in art depicting Elizabeth include a crown, sometimes a triple crown (symbolizing her life as viring, wife and widow). She is often depicted with her lap full of roses. Her feast day is 17 November.

Etheldreda [died 679]

Also known as **Audrey**, St Etheldreda was an East Anglian princess. She was married twice. Her first husband, Tondbert, gave her the Isle of Ely as a dowry and did not stand in her way when she announced that she wanted to become a nun. He died three years after they were married. Etheldreda wanted to spend the rest of her life in religious retirement, but her family forced her to marry again, this time to Ecgfrith, king of Northumbria. He was greatly devoted to her but bitterly resented the conditions of their marriage. After twelve years, he relented and gave her permission to leave him and become a nun. She took the veil at Coldingham, but after a year founded a monastery at Ely for men and women. Etheldreda became the first abbess, consecrated in that office by St WILFRID, bishop of York. As abbess, she led a life of great austerity and devotion. She wore only woollen garments, ate only once a day, and spent much time in religious observation. She died after being abbess for seven years. It is said that, when her coffin was opened sixteen years later, her body was uncorrupted. Etheldreda is said to have been very beautiful and to have inspired affection in everyone with whom she came into contact. She gained the love and admiration of two husbands, of St Wilfrid and St CUTHBERT, her nephew the king of Kent, and the nuns over whom she ruled. Her feast day is 23 June.

F

Fabian [died 250]

St Fabian was bishop of Rome. It is said that when the brothers were gathered in the church to elect their new bishop, a dove was seen to settle on Fabian's head. He was enthroned right away. Fabian was pope for sixteen years. He appointed seven deacons to write the lives of the martyrs. He was himself martyred under Decius. His feast day (with SEBASTIAN) is 20 January.

Faith [died *c*. 304]

St Faith was a virgin saint who was martyred at Agen during the persecution of Diocletian. When brought before her judges and asked of what religion she was, she replied, 'From a child I have served the Lord Jesus with all my heart, I confess His Name and commit myself to Him with entire devotion.' The magistrate urged Faith to withdraw her confession and, when she refused, ordered that she be burnt to death. It is said that her unshakeable resolve so impressed a fellow Christian, who had been watching the proceedings from a hiding place, that he came forward, confessed himself also a Christian, and shared her fate. Faith is usually represented with a palm branch and a grate. Her feast day is 6 October.

Felicitas *see* **Perpetua**.

Francis de Sales [1567–1622]

St Francis de Sales was the eldest son of the Seigneur de
Nouvelles and was born in the castle at Sales, near Annecy.
His parents were devout, and his education was carefully
planned from an early age. His favourite amusement, when
he was a child, was to summon the local children by ringing
a bell and teach them the Catechism. Francis wanted to be a
priest, but his father had other ideas. He was sent to the University of Paris, then to Padua, to study law. But he came
home in 1591 more determined than ever to be ordained. His
father gave in reluctantly, and Francis was ordained deacon
in 1597 and priest three months later. He had already been
made provost of Geneva, but defied precedent by refusing to
be also a senator so that he might give undivided service to
God. Francis made it a rule to say Mass every day and to
preach whenever the opportunity presented itself. His sermons were simple, practical and homely. He avoided controversy and argued that it was possible to withstand heresy
without being controversial. He maintained that the test of a
sermon was to be found in its practical effect on those who
heard it. He believed in short sermons: 'The more you say,
the less people remember.' He did not care about the size of
his congregations: 'I have found more real results for God's
glory when preaching to a few . . .' In 1594, the duke of Savoy asked the bishop of Geneva to send a priest to Chablais,
where the Calvinists had been dominant and the Catholic
church suppressed for nearly sixty years. Francis volun-
teered to be the one to go and, despite his father's protests,
set out on this dangerous and unpromising mission. He met
every kind of opposition, and his life was in danger on sev-

eral occasions. But his courage and gentleness triumphed in the end. When he first went, he could not say Mass in the principal town of Thonon; on Christmas Day 1596, High Mass was sung publicly and eight hundred people were present. Francis had won them over. Complaints were made to the bishop about what was seen as his excessive indulgence towards heretics. In 1599, Francis was appointed coadjutor bishop of Geneva and visited Rome. On his return, he continued to preach, and it was often said of him, as of St Stephen, that his face was like that of an angel. On one occasion, it was lit up with a halo of light. Francis spent most of the year 1602 in Paris. He preached extensively, and crowds came to hear him. Henry IV was impressed and tried to persuade Francis to remain in Paris with a number of lucrative offers, but Francis refused. He succeeded the bishop of Geneva and was consecrated in 1602. He gave away his private fortune, although the income of his see was small. He refused to build a palace, preferring to live simply in a rented house. Although he lived a life of asceticism and mortification, he never allowed those virtues to get in the way of common sense. He ruled his diocese with love and gentleness. Erring priests, sinful women and condemned criminals alike found in him love and sympathy. He was accessible to all people at all times. Children loved him, and he instituted a Catechism for children on Sunday afternoons at the cathedral of Annecy, usually conducting it himself. Before the service, a choirboy was sent round the town ringing a bell and summoning the faithful. In 1608, Francis published a book, *An Introduction to the Devout Life*, which has been an enormously popular book of devotion. This started out as a list of instructions he had written from time to time for a penitent in Paris. They had been kept, and Francis had in effect written a book without realizing it. They were rewritten at the request of Henry IV and expanded, then published. Francis could be severe and rebuke sternly when the occasion demanded. He founded the Order of the Visitation and appointed Madame de Chantal the first superior. At first the members did not take vows and spent their time visiting and nursing the sick. Later, against Francis' wishes, they became an enclosed order and took the usual vows. Although incessantly occupied with the affairs of his diocese, Francis found time to write his famous *Treatise on the Love of God*, published in 1616. Two years later he visited Paris again and stayed for a year, preaching. Worn out with all his labours, he died in 1622. His feast day is 24 January.

Francis of Assisi [1182–1226]

St Francis was born at Assisi in Italy. His father was a cloth merchant who was travelling in France when his son was born. He therefore called him Francesco (or 'the Frenchman'). His mother had been going to call him John. As a young man, Francis was full of life and was a fashionable figure among the young of Assisi. He fought in battle and was taken prisoner on one occasion. When he returned to Assisi, he fell sick with a fever and became disillusioned with his way of life up to that point. He decided to embark on a career as a soldier of fortune, but soon after setting out he was again struck down by fever. This time he made up his mind to renounce the world. He travelled to Rome, gave away all his money and changed clothes with a beggar. He then ministered to lepers. One day, he went into a little way-side chapel and there and then gave himself up to Christ. He never looked back from that decision. The ruling passion of his life became the suffering of Christ and shame for his own past sins. When Francis went back to Assisi, people thought he was a madman; children shouted at him in the street and threw stones at him. His father was furious at what his son had become and dragged Francis in front of the bishop. A crowd gathered to hear what sentence was to be passed. The bishop told Francis to give up any money he had to his father. Francis went into the house, came out naked and laid his clothes and all his possessions on the ground. He then went away covered only by an old cloak given to him by the bishop's gardener. He had not, however, decided on his future course of action. But on the Feast of St MATTHIAS, he heard Mass in the chapel of St Mary of the Angels and from then his life was marked out. He was twenty-seven. A rich gentleman of Assisi, called Bernard, was struck by Francis' meekness and humility. He offered him shelter and watched Francis at prayer. He was so impressed by Francis' devotion, that he asked Francis to let him go with him. They went to-gether to the church of St Nicholas. After Mass, they heard the words of Jesus from the missal, and Francis said, 'Brother, this is our life, and our rule, and that of all who may join us.' Bernard went out and gave away all his worldly possessions. Soon others joined them, although at first they had no fixed dwelling place. They built huts to live in, and wore the coarse brown tunics of Italian peasants, tied with a rough cord. They went about in twos and threes and often slept in haylofts or in the open air. They preached, tended the sick and lepers and begged for their food. In 1210, Francis went with eleven of his brothers to Rome to seek the pope's approval for their order. Although the pope is said to have been revolted by their dirty state, he eventually sent them away with his blessing. In 1211, they settled at Portiuncula, which was handed over to them by the Benedictines to whom it belonged. They called themselves the Poor Brothers and led a life of prayer, hard work and poverty. As far as possible, they supported themselves by the work of their hands, but begged when necessary. Their principal work was ministering to lepers, and cleaning churches. They also worked as domestic servants and olive gatherers. They observed the strictest poverty. Francis did not want the priests of the order even to own books. And he discouraged them from ever displaying sadness and depression. Like many other saints, Francis had a remarkable affinity with wild animals. He was known to preach to birds. When he rescued a hare from a trap, it ran to him and not away from him. When a fisherman, who was rowing Francis across a lake, offered him a freshly caught fish, Francis returned the fish to the water. In 1219, Francis travelled east and is said to have visited both Crusaders and Saracens in their encampments. He was venerated by everyone. Later, he visited the Holy Land and obtained special permission from the sultan to see the Holy Sepulchre. When he returned to his order, he was saddened to learn that the brothers wanted to move away from his original intention and towards less emphasis on poverty and a closer resemblance to the longer established monastic foundations. They wanted a more elaborate rule, regular hours, the admission of pupils. Both his friend and patron, Cardinal Ugolini, and the

Roman court urged these changes on Francis. So, although the last years of his life were overshadowed by the thought that his original idea was being destroyed, he reluctantly agreed to the desired changes and, in 1220, resigned the office of superior of the order. His last years were, therefore, spent in protest that almost everything being done in the order was against his wishes or without his knowledge. In 1224, Francis retreated to a lonely spot in the Apennine mountains for forty days of fasting. On his way, while he rested under a tree, small birds settled on his head and shoulders, and around his feet. They sang and flapped their wings, and Francis took this as a sign that it pleased Christ that he should live on his lonely mountain. He began his fast and was much troubled by temptations from the Devil. On 14 September, Holy Cross Day, the Stigmata appeared on his hands and feet, and Christ appeared to him on the Cross and endorsed Francis as his standard-bearer. Francis was filled with great joy and then, when the vision disappeared, with great pain, and he saw the marks of Christ in his hands and feet. He returned to Portiuncula, where he succumbed to an eye complaint that required painful surgery. On the night before his operation, Francis spent some time in a cell of reeds made by St Clare in her convent garden, where mice ran over and around him, denying him prayer and rest. He underwent the treatment, which was unsuccessful, and he returned to Assisi to die. When told by doctors that death was near, Francis asked brothers to come and sing to him his own hymn of praise, *Song of Brother Sun*, which they did day and night. He was carried to Portiuncula on a litter and blessed Assisi for the last time. He died on 3 October, and it is said that a multitude of larks flew round the roof of the house where he lay and sang sweetly as if praising the Lord with St Francis. His emblems include the stimata, the lily for purity, and a skull, a reminder of mortality. His feast day is 4 October.

Francis Xavier [1506–1552]

St Francis Xavier was the youngest son of a Spanish nobleman of Navarre. He was more interested in an academic than a military life, and went to study at the University of Paris when he was seventeen. He was a distinguished student and was made Master of Arts in 1530. He taught logic and metaphysics, and among those who attended his lectures was IGNATIUS LOYOLA, who was anxious to make friends with Francis. Initially, Francis treated Ignatius coldly and with suspicion, but he was eventually won over and was one of the six companions who took vows at Montmartre and were the original Jesuits. After he had spent some time in Rome, Francis was told by Ignatius to go with Simon Rodriguez on a mission to the East Indies. Francis confessed to Simon that he had foretold this journey in a dream and knew what was in store. He sailed from Lisbon on 17 April 1541, the day Ignatius was elected the first general of the Society of Jesus. The ship had more than nine hundred people on board and, although they were uncongenial company, Francis mixed freely with them. His tendency to rub shoulders and talk with all and sundry scandalized some of his peers, but also led to the reforming of many more. He was adept at patching up quarrels, nursed the sick, heard confessions and preached. The voyage lasted thirteen months, including a stay of six months in Mozambique. They landed at Goa in India in 1542, where Francis took on the enormous task of caring for the Portuguese officials and merchants, their wives and children, as well as converting the native Indians. During the six years that followed, Francis visited the Portuguese settlements and sailed east as far as the Celebes and Molucca islands. His approach to converting the native population was to have the Catechism and prayers and hymns translated into the local vernacular. He would stay for several weeks, teaching the children and some of their parents to sing what he had taught them. When he moved on, he left a native teacher to continue the instruction. He would go through the streets ringing a bell to summon the children to his lessons, and he called on all who would come and learn the Christian doctrine. Later, each centre was visited regularly by himself or another Jesuit. Francis had enormous influence, and he sometimes baptised so many that he could hardly lift his hands. He regarded baptism as the most important part of a missionary's work. He is said to have had a remarkable gift for languages, and many miracles are attributed to him. He was very austere. He travelled barefoot, wearing a torn cassock and with a black cap on his head. He ate only once a day, and then only rice. He seldom slept for more than four hours, and he lay on the bare ground with a stone for a pillow. The rest of the night was spent in prayer or tending the sick. He is credited with converting some of the most unpromising characters. But Francis was a man of affairs as well as a mystic. Many of his letters that survive deal with practical matters. They contain advice on preaching and on administering rebukes to highly placed officials, but also on the admission of recruits to the society and managing finances (including how to recover borrowed money). He even dealt with the housekeeping and the gardening. No detail was too small. Like FRANCIS OF ASSISI, Francis Xavier is said to have had an affinity with animals. He resolved to visit Japan. This voyage was his most dangerous as, apart from the usual dangers of the sea, he and his companions risked being thrown overboard as bringers of bad luck if their ship met unfavourable winds. Despite all the dangers, Francis landed at Kagoshima in 1549. He stayed there for about two years. He met considerable opposition and was wounded by arrows, pelted with mud and almost stoned to death. He and his companions were often followed by a jeering crowd. But, although progress was slow and difficult, many converts were made, and most converts appear to have remained faithful. One Jesuit told of visiting a place where he had baptised fifteen people twelve years earlier, and which had not been visited by a priest since. He found these same people faithful and eager for news of Father Francis. He had many disputes with Japanese officials and always made a point, when writing home, that it was necessary to send able and learned men as missionaries to Japan, where Francis was first to preach the Gospel. He set off on a return voyage to India in 1551, having already decided that China would be his next port of call. He set sail early the following year. After stopping at Singapore, he reached the island of San Chan, one hundred and twenty miles from Canton. While waiting for an opportunity to get into Canton, he fell ill with a fever and died aboard his ship, the *Santa Croce*. His feast day is 3 December.

Frideswide [died *c.* 730]

St Frideswide was the daughter of a Mercian prince who lived at Oxford. While still quite young, she became a nun and founded a convent. Attracted by reports of her beauty, a neighbouring prince, Algar, sought her hand in marriage. When she refused him, he invaded Oxford with an army. According to one story, he was struck by blindness, but his sight was restored after Frideswide's intercession. Frideswide fled from Oxford, with two nuns, in a boat rowed by an angel. They took refuge in the woods near Abingdon. They stayed there for some time, and it is said that a fountain sprang up at her prayer. On her return to Oxford, Frideswide met a leper who begged her to kiss him. This she did, and his leprosy was cured. She lived in her convent and devoted herself to working among the poor and the wretched. She nursed the sick and taught the ignorant. Later her convent was given to the Augustinians, was acquired by Cardinal Wolsey for his college and, after his fall, it became Christ Church. The chapel, rebuilt in the twelfth century, is the present cathedral. For centuries, Frideswide's tomb was one of the most popular places of pilgrimage in England. It was robbed by Henry VIII. In the next reign, her bones were cast out and replaced by those of Peter Martyr the Reformer. Queen Mary restored them and expelled those of her successor. In the reign of Queen Elizabeth, these were in turn replaced and now both lie in the tomb. Her feast day is 19 October.

G

George [died 303]

St George was born in Palestine. He was a soldier who became a tribune in the Imperial Guard. He left the army and dedicated himself to fighting the cause of his fellow Christians who were being persecuted by the Roman emperor, Diocletian. After freeing his slaves, selling everything he owned and giving away all his money, he set off to see the emperor. On the way, at Beirut, he is thought to have met and killed a crocodile—the 'dragon' that, in the popular imagination, George is reputed to have slain. It is possible that the dragon—a symbol of paganism—and his slaying of it represent the conversion of a heathen country to Christianity. When he reached the imperial court, his pleas to the emperor were in vain, and George himself stood accused of allegiance to Christ and was tortured and beheaded. He was buried at Lydda in Palestine, and a church was later built above his tomb by the emperor Constantine. St George is thought to have visited England, and his reputation was enhanced by English crusaders. He is the patron saint of England and of the Italian city of Genoa, and also of soldiers and sailors. He is the protector of rocky coasts and of areas at risk of flooding, and is particularly associated with the rose. His emblem is a red cross on a white ground (the English flag). His feast day is 23 April.

German [c. 378–448]

Also known as **Germanus**, St German was the son of Christian parents from Auxerre. He was educated in Rome then joined the imperial service and rose through the ranks, becoming one of the six governors of Gaul. His territory stretched to Armorica (Brittany), but he made Auxerre his headquarters. He was passionately devoted to hunting, and his habit of hanging the heads of the animals he killed on a tree scandalized his Christian neighbours. This was a heathen custom and the bishop remonstrated with German, but to no avail. When German was away from the town, the bishop had the tree cut down and its trophies disposed of. When he was forty, and in accordance with tradition, German was ordained priest by force and against his will. Shortly afterwards, he was made bishop. From then on he was a changed man. He devoted himself to the work of Christ and became zealous and active in the performance of his duties. He was most devout and austere in his personal life. He was particularly noted for the care and knowledge with which he gave alms. In 429, alarmed by the spread of Pelagianism, the British bishops sent to the church in Gaul for help. In response, German and Lupus of Troyes were dispatched on a mission. After a stormy voyage, they landed in Britain, it is said at St Germain's in Cornwall. They preached in churches, in the streets and in the fields. The faithful were confirmed, and those who had strayed returned. At first their principal opponents remained in the background, but later agreed to meet the missionaries for a conference. This was probably held at Verulam (modern St Albans). The supporters of Pelagius (who denied man's need of divine grace) were totally defeated by the eloquence and the arguments of the two bishops who, for good measure, confirmed their superiority by restoring the sight of a blind girl. A chapel dedicated to St German was built close to the ruins of the ancient Verulam. After the conference, German and Lupus visited the tomb of St ALBAN. German deposited relics of the Apostles and took away some dust from the spot where the martyr had been put to death. Shortly afterwards, the Britons were called upon to repel a raid mounted by their old enemies the Picts and the Scots. Their courage had been sorely tested by several defeats, and they summoned German and Lupus to their side, and the two bishops inspired new courage in the troops. During the march, they preached daily and baptised most of the army. They put up a rough wattle church in which to celebrate Easter. When the enemy were known to be nearby, German appears to have regained some of his early soldiering instincts, and he elected himself leader of the British army. He arranged an ambush—at a prearranged signal, there was a universal cry of 'Alleluia!' and the enemy fled in panic. The Britons did not lose a single man. The encounter is said to have taken place near Mold (in Wales), and the church in the next parish is dedicated to St German—it is possibly on the spot where the wattle church was built. After this victory, German returned to France. Seventeen years later he once again visited Britain, when he heard that the Pelagian heresy was reviving. But he found the people constant in their faith and did not feel it necessary to stay. Almost immediately after this, German was called on to intercede for the Armoricans who had been sentenced for rebellion. He travelled to Ravenna to plead their cause before the emperor. After being received with great honour and respect, German died at Ravenna in 448. His feast day is 31 July.

Germanus *see* **German**.

Gertrude [died 664]
St Gertrude was born into a Frankish noble family. She was Charlemagne's great-aunt. As a child, she resolved to dedicate herself to Christ. When she was fourteen, her father died, and Gertrude and her mother retired to a convent at Nivelles. After twelve years, she succeeded her mother as abbess of the community. She built churches and hospitals for widows and orphans, and rest houses for pilgrims and other travellers. She became the patron saint of travellers (*see also* CHRISTOPHER), and was later believed to harbour souls on their way to heaven, and to protect departed spirits. St Gertrude is usually represented with a mouse, on the grounds that she was frequently so absorbed in prayer that a mouse could have run up her staff and she would not have noticed. Her feast day is 17 March.

Giles [sixth or eighth century]
Also known as **Aegidius**, St Giles is thought to have been born in Athens. The dates of his life are uncertain, his biographer describing him as a contemporary of two figures who lived two hundred years apart. On his way to Rome, Giles stayed with the bishop of Arles and left him to become a hermit on the banks of the Rhone. One day, Flavius, king of the Goths, was hunting and came upon Giles in his cave. The hermit stood at the mouth of the cave and was accidentally wounded by an arrow. The king ordered that Giles and the

hind they had been hunting be left unmolested. The king revisited the cave in the days that followed and had many con-
versations with Giles, who advised him to build a monastery.
The king agreed on condition that Giles become the first abbot, which he reluctantly consented to. Giles is the patron
saint of cripples and beggars. He was particularly popular in
England in the Middle Ages when more than a hundred and
fifty churches were dedicated to him. His emblems are the
stag and the arrow. His feast day is 1 September.

Gregory I [*c.* 540–604]

Also called **Gregory the Great**, St Gregory was born into a
rich and noble Roman family and was brought up to follow a
career in the law. He was so proficient that, at the age of
thirty, he was appointed prefect of the city and became one
of the most important figures of his day. For reasons that are
not recorded, Gregory decided to give up his prominent position and become a monk. With the money he inherited on his
father's death, he founded six Benedictine monasteries in
Sicily and a seventh, dedicated to St ANDREW, in Rome. This
last he entered as a novice. Gregory embraced the austerities
of the religious life with such zeal that his health suffered
and he was afflicted by stomach pains for the rest of his life.
Soon after becoming a monk, Gregory obtained the pope's
permission to travel to Britain as a missionary, but only three
days into his journey he was compelled to return by popular
demand. Some years later, when he was abbot of St
Andrew's, he organized huge processions that crossed Rome
for three whole days singing litanies against the plague. At
the end of the three days, Gregory is said to have seen an an-

gel sheath his sword as a signal that the plague was ended. In 590, much against his will, Gregory was elected pope. He complained of the burdens of that office, but he worked remarkably hard and was a most painstaking administrator. Many of his letters survive and bear this out. No detail was too small for his personal attention, and he still found time to preach and write books. He personally trained a choir and reformed the ecclesiastical music of the day, giving his name to the tones known as 'Gregorian'. His theological writings rank him with Saints AMBROSE, AUGUSTINE OF HIPPO and JEROME. Gregory was very charitable and daily provided for a horde of beggars. He even held himself responsible when a man died of starvation in Rome, and did penance as though he were guilty of a sin. Every night he entertained twelve guests to supper. One night, there appeared to be thirteen and, later, Gregory discovered that he had entertained an angel unawares. He sent AUGUSTINE to England in 596 and took the greatest interest in his mission. He provided the infant English church with books, vestments, relics and a steady relay of missionaries. After suffering years of ill health, St Gregory finally succumbed and died in 604. His emblem is a dove. His feast day is 3 September.

Gregory VII [c. 1020–1085]
Gregory, whose monastic name was **Hildebrand**, was born in southern Tuscany. He spent his youth in Rome, in the monastery of St Maria, of which his uncle, Laurentius (afterwards bishop of Amalfi) was abbot. After Rome he went to the celebrated monastery at Cluny where he completed his education and acquired his adherence to strict ascetic ob-

servances, which he practised his whole life. He visited the court of Henry III, and his preaching gained him a reputation for eloquence. He was a protege of Gregory VI, whom he accompanied into exile to Germany. After the death of Gregory VI in 1048, Hildebrand probably returned to Cluny, but at the request of the new pope, Leo IX, he accompanied him to Rome in 1049. Under this active and devoted pontiff Hildebrand exercised great influence and was eventually created cardinal. Besides his normal responsibilities, he was sent as legate to the Council of Tours. Under the short pontificates of the successors of Leo IX—Victor II, Stephen IX, Benedict X and Alexander II—Hildebrand continued to exercise the same influence. On the death of Alexander II in 1073 he was elected pope, but the German bishops, who feared the effect of his reforms, tried to prevent Emperor Henry IV from assenting to the election, but Henry gave his approval, and the new pope was crowned in 1073. Gregory believed that the welfare of the church and the regeneration of society were inseparably linked. He regarded as evil the thoroughly secularized condition of the church, especially in Germany and northern Italy, and he directed all his efforts towards reforming abuses in the church, establishing papal supremacy and abolishing lay investiture. The year after his election he prohibited this practice, under pain of excommunication, and in the following year he issued that sentence against several bishops and councillors. Emperor Henry IV took the bishops under his protection, and Gregory cited him to Rome to answer for his conduct. Henry's reply was to defy, and in a diet at Worms in 1076 he formally declared Gregory deposed. Gregory retaliated by excommunicating

Henry, and as this sentence involved the forfeiture of all civil rights and the loss of all civil and political offices, Henry's Saxon subjects compelled him to yield. By doing penance at Canossa in 1077, Henry obtained absolution from the pope in person. But this submission was short-lived, and following his subsequent triumph over his rival, Ruldolf of Swabia, Henry resumed hostilities with the pope, and in 1080 again declared him deposed and caused Guibert, archbishop of Ravenna, to be appointed in his place as Clement III. After a three year siege, Henry captured Rome in 1084. Gregory shut himself up in the castle of St Angelo but was rescued by Robert Guiscard, the Norman duke of Apulia, who compelled Henry to return to Germany. Gregory left Rome, first for Monte Cassino and ultimately to Salerno, where he died. His dying words were, 'I have loved justice and hated iniquity; therefore I die an exile.' His feast day is 25 May.

Gregory Nazianzens [c. 330–c. 390]

Gregory was born at Arianzus, a village near Nazianzus in Cappadocia, not far from Caesarea in Palestine. His father originally belonged to a heathen sect but became a convert to Christianity about the time of the Nicene Council in 325, and four years later was made bishop of Nazianzus. At an early age Gregory was sent to study at Caesarea before attending the schools of Alexandria and (about 348–358) Athens, where he met BASIL, then also a young student, and became his most intimate friend. Gregory made brilliant progress in rhetoric, philosophy and sacred literature and returned to Nazianzus, where in 360 he was baptised by his father and consecrated to God all 'his goods, his glory, his health, his tongue, and his talents'. To prepare themselves for a life of austere devotion, he and Basil lived in the desert near the River Iris in Pontus. Recalled by his father, Gregory was ordained priest but afterwards fled. Recalled a second time, he returned to Nazianzus, assisted his father in the ministry, and preached. About 372 Basil, who had become bishop of Caesarea, prevailed upon him to accept the see of Sasima, a small town in Cappadocia. Scarcely had he taken on this office, however, than he was overcome again by his innate repugnance to public life, and he retired, a bishop wihout a bishopric, to Nazianzus, where he stayed until the death of his father in 374. He then went into a monastery at Seleucia, but in 378 he was persuaded to leave it to join a small Nicene congregation in Constantinople, where, until then, Arianism had held undisputed sway. Soon his erudition and rhetoric became conspicuous, and he was elected archbishop, exasperating the Arians to such an extent that his life was in danger. Although upheld by Pope Damasus and Emperor Theodosius, Gregory resigned his see voluntarily 'in order to lay the storm, like another Jonah, although he had not excited it'. He went back to Nazianzus and a solitary life near Arianzus until he died. His ashes were taken to Constantinople, and then, during the crusades, to Rome. His feast day is (with Basil) is 2 January.

Gregory of Nyssa [331–395]

Gregory was the younger brother of BASIL. After being educated by his brother, he showed an inclination to become a teacher of rhetoric, but was influenced by GREGORY NAZIANZENS to devote himself to the church. He was consecrated by

Basil bishop of Nyssa, in Cappadocia, in 371 or 372. During the persecution of the adherents of the Nicene Creed, in the reign of Valens, Gregory was deposed by a synod held in Galatia on the pretext that he had wasted the church's goods. After the death of Valens he was welcomed back in 378. He was present at the Council of Constantinople in 381, and (along with two other bishops) was appointed to oversee the diocese of Pontus. He travelled to Arabia and Jerusalem to set in order the churches there, and was again at a synod in Constantinople in 394. He probably died soon afterwards. Of the three Cappadocians Gregory was the greatest speculative theologian, the most faithful to Origenistic views, and not the least zealous defender of Nicene doctrine. He was a less able ruler than Basil, who sometimes lamented his untimely 'good nature' and 'simplicity'. His feast day is 9 March.

Gregory of Tours [*c.* 540–594]

Gregory was born at Arverna (now Clermont), the chief town of Auvergne, and belonged to one of the most distinguished Roman families of Gaul. Originally called Georgius Florentius, he assumed the name Gregory out of respect for his mother's grandfather, Gregory, bishop of Langres. He was educated by his uncle, Gallus, bishop of Clermont, and after his death by Avitus, a priest of his native town. His recovery from a severe sickness, through a pilgrimage to the grave of St Martin of Tours, led him to devote himself to the church. His election as bishop of Tours in 573 was favoured by Sigbert, king of Austrasia, to whom Auvergne had fallen on the death of Clothar I in 561. In the struggles for Tours between Sigbert and his wife Brunhilda on the one side against

Chilperic and his wife Fredegond on the other, he took the side of the former, and in the course of the conflict in which the city frequently changed hands he had to suffer many persecutions. After the death of Chilperic, whom Gregory called 'the Nero and Herod of our time', he enjoyed great influence over his successors, Guntram and Childebert II. He wrote a *History of the Franks* to which we owe our exact knowledge of the dark and stormy times of the Merovingian kings. His feast day is 17 November.

Gregory Thaumaturgus [*c.* 210–*c.* 270]
Gregory, also called **Gregory the Wonder-worker**, was born the son of wealthy heathen parents at Neocaesarea, in Pontus, and was originally named Theodorus. His early education was for the law, but he came under the influence of the Christian scholar Origen at Caesarea in Palestine and was his disciple for about eight years, with an interruption caused by the persecution under Maximin, during which he probably studied at Alexandria. On his return to his homeland, he was consecrated bishop of Neocaesarea. His influence in Asia Minor continued from the middle of the third century to far down into the fourth, and its extent may be inferred from the numerous legends of his miracles and the tradition that at the time of his death there were only as many pagans in Neocaesarea as there had been Christians in it at his consecration—seventeen. His *Ekthesis*, or 'Confession of Faith', said to have been derived by revelation from the Virgin MARY and the apostle JOHN, is a summary of Origen's theology and is of value as a record of the state of theology at the middle of the third century. His feast day is 17 November.

H

Helena [*c*. 248–327]

St Helena was the daughter of an innkeeper and was the mother of Constantine the Great, the first Christian emperor. She is said to have become a Christian herself under the influence of her son and, at the age of eighty, to have made a pilgrimage to Rome, possibly to atone for the sins of Constantine, who had murdered his son and his wife. Helena gave large sums of money to the poor and used her powerful position to secure the release of prisoners and the return of exiles. She is said to have built churches on the sites of the Passion, the Resurrection and the Ascension, and during her visit to Rome to have discovered the wood of the Cross. All three crosses were found, and there was no way of telling which was the one on which Christ had died. At Helena's suggestion, a piece of wood from each was brought to the bedside of a sick woman. Two had no effect on her at all, but in the presence of the wood from the third cross, the woman recovered completely and it was thereby established which was the true Cross. Symbols associated with St Helena are a cross, three nails, and a hammer. Her feast day is 18 August.

Hilary of Arles [*c*. 403–449]

Hilary was born in Arles and educated at the celebrated mo-

nastic school of Lerins, and was made bishop of his native
city in 429. He presided at several synods, especially at Or-
ange in 441, the proceedings of which involved him in a serious controversy with Pope Leo I who overturned his deposi-
tion of two bishops. Hilary, however, refused to submit to the
decision. He did not question the authority in itself, but he
maintained that it was uncanonically exercised. In the end,
however, he sought a reconciliation with Pope Leo, and the
dispute was brought to an amicable end. His feast day was
formerly 5 May.

Hilary of Poitiers [died 368]

St Hilary was born at Poitiers. His parents were pagans, and
he was an adult before he was converted. He seems to have
been chosen bishop of Poitiers while a layman, and he had a
wife when he was consecrated but did not live with her after
his ordination. Hilary was famous as a teacher. St MARTIN
came to Poitiers to hear him preach and became his disciple.
Hilary was noted for his strenuous opposition to the Arians.
He was banished in 356. During the period of his banishment, he wrote hymns and treatises against the Arians. After
four years, he was allowed to return. In 363, Hilary visited
Italy and had a public dispute with the Arian bishop of Milan. Most of his episcopate was devoted to defending his
faith. His feast day is 13 January.

Hilda [614–680]

St Hilda was born into a royal family. Her father was murdered, and she lived at the court of her great-uncle Edwin,

who was king of Northumbria. She was influenced by St
PAULINUS and her aunt Ethelburga, and was baptised at York
on the eve of Easter when she was thirteen. Hilda had intended to go to a convent in France, but AIDAN persuaded her
to stay in Northumbria. It is believed he put her in charge of a
small religious community on the banks of the River Tweed.
She then became abbess of the monastery at Hartlepool
where Aidan frequently visited her. After a number of years,
Hilda founded a monastery at Whitby for men and women. It
soon became famous as a school. She was one of the principal champions of the Celtic usages when they were debated
at the Synod of Whitby, which was held at her monastery.
Although it was contrary to her own beliefs, she accepted the
synod's ruling, which went against her. Hilda ruled her monastery with great diligence and was a noted patron of learning. Five pupils of hers became bishops. She was so widely
known for her wisdom that kings and princes visited her
seeking her advice. For the last six years of her life, St Hilda
suffered from a lingering disease, which she bore with great
patience and courage. It is said that on the night she died, a
nun, thirteen miles away, saw the top of Hilda's house open
and a strange light appear. In the light. The nun saw Hilda's
soul being carried to heaven by angels. Frightened, the nun
called the sister who was in charge. All the sisters were summoned to the church and spent the night praying and singing
psalms for Hilda's soul. When monks came from Whitby
next day to bring news that Hilda had died, they found the
news was already known. It was established that Hilda had
died at the moment when the vision was seen. Her feast day
is 17 November.

Hildebrand *see* **Gregory VII**.

Hugh of Avalon [*c*. 1135–1200]
Also known as **Hugh of Lincoln,** St Hugh was born into a
noble Burgundian family. On the death of Hugh's mother, his
father retired to a monastery and took Hugh, then aged eight,
with him to be brought up as a monk. It seems that this had
always been Hugh's destiny. He had never indulged in child-
ish pleasures and games, and, even in the monastery school,
he was not allowed to play with other boys. When he was a
deacon, he went with his prior to the monastery of the
Grande Chartreuse. He so admired the rigid discipline and
complete separation from the world that he sought admission
into the community. He was a monk there for fifteen years,
during which time he was noted, in an austere ambience, for
his even greater austerity. He wore a hair shirt and took only
bread and water as nourishment. His health suffered consid-
erably as a result. He was appointed procurator and won eve-
rybody's admiration. At about this time, Henry II had tried to
establish a Carthusian monastery at Witham in Somerset.
The first prior had left without permission, the second had
died, and Henry's enterprise seemed doomed to failure.
Word reached him of Hugh, and he sent the bishop of Bath to
ask Hugh to become the next prior of Witham. Much against
his will, Hugh was sent to take up this post. Immediately a
rapport between Henry and Hugh was firmly established,
with Hugh apparently able to address the king more frankly
and directly than anyone else dared. Hugh was often critical
of Henry. Hugh was made bishop of Lincoln. He incurred the
king's displeasure by excommunicating the chief forester.

Hugh and Henry quarrelled but their differences were patched up. Hugh had a similar relationship with Richard I. His relations with King John, however, were less happy. One Easter, Hugh preached at some length. John was displeased by the length of the discourse and three times ordered Hugh to bring it to a close. Hugh ignored these instructions, and the king left without taking communion. Hugh was a diligent and wise ruler of his huge diocese. He gathered about him men of learning in Lincoln. The cathedral was begun and parts of it completed under his supervision. He insisted on a high standard of conduct among the clergy. He had simple tastes and hated ostentatious displays. When he travelled to Winchester to be consecrated, he insisted on carrying his luggage strapped behind his saddle, to the great distress of his chaplains. He devoted much time to caring for the sick, especially lepers whose sores he washed with his own hands. He insisted on taking funerals himself if he thought fit. He even kept King Richard waiting on one occasion while he buried someone who had died. Hugh was adept at settling quarrels and disputes. He loved peace and hated injustice. He was moderate and frugal in his diet, yet he scolded monks who practised abstinence beyond what was required by their vows. Many miracles were attributed to him, but it seems Hugh attached no particular importance to them. He was an insatiable collector of relics, although he sometimes used questionable methods to obtain them. Like many saints, Hugh loved animals. Whenever he could, he would escape to Witham for a few days or weeks to live as a simple monk. He fell sick in London in September 1200. On 16 November, he sent for the monks of Westminster and the clerks of St Paul's to chant compline. He was lifted from his bed and laid on a cross of ashes on the floor. As the choir sang, Hugh died. He was buried at Lincoln Cathedral. Crowds followed his body out of London and struggled to touch the bier. Miracles marked the stages of this last journey. His body was met outside Lincoln by the kings of England and Scotland and such an assembly of bishops and abbots as had never been seen in England before, as well as a vast crowd of lay folk of every kind. The body has never been moved. St Hugh is usually represented with a swan. He was canonized in 1280. His feast day is 17 November.

I

Ignatius of Antioch [died 107]

A legend of the Middle Ages says that Ignatius was the child
that Jesus took up in his arms and showed to the disciples as
a symbol of humility. As bishop of Antioch he succeeded
Evodius, who had succeeded St PETER. His surname was
Theophorus, which means 'one who carries God in his
heart'. Ignatius occupied the see of Antioch for forty years,
until Emperor Trajan resumed the persecution of the church
as an act of gratitude to his gods for his victories. Ignatius
was condemned to be taken to Rome and thrown to wild
beasts. Wherever the ship touched land, Christians flocked to
receive the blessing of the bishop, whom they already
viewed as a martyr. The letters he wrote on his journey give a
clear picture of church government under bishops, priests
and deacons. The last stages of the journey were hurried so
that he would arrive in Rome before the public games ended.
He was devoured by two large lions in the amphitheatre, and
the remaining largest bones were wrapped in silk and taken
back to Antioch. His feast day is 17 October.

Ignatius of Loyola [c. 1495–1556]

St Ignatius was a Spaniard, born in the Castle of Loyola near
Azpeitia. He was probably the youngest of thirteen children

of a noble family. He became a soldier and, at the siege of Pamplona, received a severe bullet wound in his leg, which altered the course of his life. During his convalescence he asked for a copy of *Amadis of Gaul*, a fashionable romance of the period, but he was given instead the *Flower of the Saints* and the *Life of Christ* by Ludolph, a Carthusian. At first he read idly but soon found himself in a deep spiritual conflict, torn between his desire for the pleasures of the world and the spirituality of the religious life. He chose the latter. His new way of life was confirmed by a vision of the Virgin Mary with the infant Christ in her arms, which appeared to him one night in a blaze of light. He decided to make a pilgrimage to the shrine of Our Lady of Montserrat, and stayed for nearly a year at nearby Manresa. There he practised the most severe mortifications, sometimes going for a week without food, and his health never completely recovered. He composed the famous *Spiritual Exercises*, a course of meditations for those wishing to develop their spiritual life. Ignatius begged his way to the Holy Land, reaching Jerusalem in 1523. He would have stayed there, but the guardian of the holy places became alarmed at his attempts to convert Moslems and commanded him to leave. He returned to Barcelona and became a student, studying first at Alcala and then at Salamanca, but at each university he got into trouble with the Inquisition and left without finishing his course. He then went to the University of Paris, where he stayed for seven years, gathering round him a small band of disciples that included St Francis Xavier. On the feast of the Assumption, at the chapel of St Denis de Montmartre, they vowed to serve God in any way the pope might command

them. They resolved to make a pilgrimage to Jerusalem and
then go on to Rome to place themselves at the service of the
pope. On his way to Rome, Ignatius had a vision of Jesus,
carrying a heavy cross, surrounded by an aura of light, and
this persuaded him to call his brotherhood the Society of Jesus, or Jesuits. Pope Paul III received the men—ten in
number—kindly, and those who were not already priests
were ordained. Ignatius' military training had a strong influence on the constitution of the society: its head, to whom ab-
solute obedience was due, was called the general. The society was to be an army at the disposal of the pope for the
propagation of the faith in any part of the world. In 1541,
Ignatius was unanimously elected the first general of the order, and his first act was to appoint himself cook, an office he
held for many years. He remained in Rome for the rest of his
life, supervising the work of his growing order, while the
brethren travelled abroad on missionary work. They were
told to visit the sick and poor, and to avoid argument and displays of learning. Ignatius founded orphanages, a house for
converted Jews under instruction, and another for fallen
women. He directed his order for fifteen years, seeing it grow
from ten members to one thousand. He died suddenly in
1556, was beatified soon afterwards, and canonized in 1628.
His emblem is a heart crowned with thorns, the sacred, heart,
which is the emblem of the Jesuits. His feast day is 31 July.

Irenaeus of Lyons [c. 130–c. 200]

Irenaeus was probably born near Smyrna, in Asia Minor, and
in his early youth was aquainted with POLYCARP, but he is
kown in history solely through his connection with the

Graeco-Gaulish Church of southern France, of which he was a bishop. He was a priest of the church of Lyons, under Bishop Pothinus and after his martyrdom in 177, during the persecution of Marcus Aurelius, Irenaeus was elected to the same see, which he continued to govern for twenty-five years. He was a devout and successful missionary bishop, but his name is associated chiefly with his activity in opposing the Gnostics and with his attempts to prevent a rupture between the Eastern and Western Churches over the question of the day on which Easter was to be kept. His feast day is 28 June.

Isidore of Seville [c. 560–636]

Also called **Isidorus Hispalensis**, he was born in Seville and became archbishop of Seville about 590 and became one of the most distinguished ecclesiastics of his time. During his episcopate there were two notable half-ecclesiastical, half-civil councils at Seville in 618 or 619 and at Toledo in 633, which were held under his presidency. The canons promulgated by these may almost be said to have formed the basis of the constitutional law of the Spanish kingdoms, for both church and state, down to the great constitutional changes of the fifteenth century. Also a historian, he collected all the decrees of councils and other church laws before his time. He was noted for his simplicity and goodness. His feast day is 4 April.

J

James (first century)

St James, Jesus' brother, may have been the son of JOSEPH by a former marriage. He took a leading part in the Church of Jerusalem and became the first bishop of that place. He decided how far the Gentiles should conform to Jewish customs, pronouncing it unnecessary, for example, that they be circumcised. He was called 'the Just', because of his fairness, and it was said that his knees were as hard as a camel's because he spent so much time praying in the temple. St James made many conversions, and the scribes and pharisees came to look on him as their most dangerous opponent. Having failed to persuade him to recant publicly, he was condemned to be stoned to death. While lying half-dead, he was put out of his agony with a club called a fuller's bat, which is now the emblem with which he is represented. The siege of Jerusalem, which followed soon afterwards, was considered by many, even among the Jews, to have been a judgement on them for this crime. He was the author of the Epistle of St James. His feast day is 23 October.

James the Great [died 43]

St James the Great was the son of Zebedee and Salome, and the brother of St JOHN THE EVANGELIST. He was also a cousin of Jesus. He was a fisherman who, with his brother and his partners, St PETER and St ANDREW, left his work when Jesus called them to follow him. With Peter and John, James was chosen by Jesus to be a witness at his Transfiguration and at Gethsemane, giving the three a certain precedence among the twelve Apostles. About fourteen years after the Crucifixion, James became the first of the Apostles to be martyred, being beheaded by order of Herod Agrippa I, to appease the Jewish opponents of Christianity. His accuser was so moved by his courage during his trial that he became a Christian and was condemned himself, dying with James. St James was buried in Jerusalem, but his remains were taken to Galicia, and later to Compostela, where his shrine became a famous place of pilgrimage in the Middle Ages. He became the patron saint of Spain, and was believed to have appeared on many occasions mounted on a white horse, leading the Spanish armies to victory against the Moors. The first of these occasions was in 939, when King Ramirez of Castile vowed to deliver his country from the tribute of one hundred virgins that it was compelled to pay each year to the Moors. He collected his forces but was defeated at Clavigo. But that night, St James appeared to him, promising victory the next day. The next day, as the soldiers charged, they saw St James mounted on a white horse and waving a white standard. A great victory was won, and 60,000 Moors were left dead on the field. St James is represented with a sword, and sometimes with a pilgrim's staff and scallop shells. He is the patron saint of pilgrims. His feast day is 25 July.

Januarius [died *c.* 305]

Januarius was a native of Benevento, or at least became

bishop of that see in the later part of the third century. According to Neapolitan tradition, he was taken prisoner at Nola during the persecution of the Christians by Diocletion and was martyred at Pozzuoli, where many Christians suffered the same fate. His body and head are preserved in the cathedral at Naples, and two phials there are supposed to contain his blood. On three festivals each year, chief of which is the day of his martyrdom (19 September, the others being the first Sunday evening in May and the 16 December, as well as on occasions of public danger or calamity, such as earthquakes or eruptions) the head and the phials of the blood are carried in solemn procession to the high altar of the cathedral, where, after prayers, the blood in the phials are brought into contact with the head and is believed to liquefy. Occasionally a considerable time elapses before the liquefaction takes place, and sometimes it fails altogether. The latter is regarded as an extremely bad omen. On the occasions when the miracle is delayed beyond the ordinary time, the alarm of the congregation rises to a high pitch. His feast day is 19 September.

Jerome [331–419]

St Jerome was born into a wealthy family at Stridon, on the borders of Dalmatia and Italy. He became a doctor and one of the most learned of the early Christians. He was taught at home before being sent to study under the pagan grammarian Donatus. Although he was baptised in Rome when he was eighteen, he was still addicted to reading the great pagan writers. He set out to complete his education by travelling, but had not got far when he became converted to Christianity and decided instead to set out for the Holy Land with two companions. At Antioch, they all became ill, and his friends died. Jerome recovered and resolved to give up reading pagan authors and to devote himself to the study of divinity. He managed only to keep the latter part of this resolution. Jerome withdrew to the wilderness of Chalcis, near Antioch, where he lived alone, suffering from bad health and the great heat. To save himself from sensual thoughts, he began the study of Hebrew. After two or three years he emerged from his retreat and was ordained priest at Antioch. He then travelled to Constantinople, where he studied under GREGORY NAZIANZENS, one of the great Greek doctors of the Church, whom he revered most of all his teachers. In Rome, in 382, Pope DAMASUS made him his secretary, and he revised the Latin translation of the New Testament and of the Psalms. Although the Romans were impressed by his honesty and holiness, Jerome was disliked for his sarcasm and his contempt for his opponents. His withering attacks on the failings of Roman society made him many enemies, and on the death of his protector, Damasus, in 385, Jerome left Rome. He was followed by a group of Roman women who wished to lead a religious life. A small monastery was built in Bethlehem, near the basilica of the Nativity, as well as buildings to house three communities of women and a cell in which St Jerome lived and worked. Here, he accomplished his greatest work, the Latin translation of the Bible, known as the Vulgate. After the sacking of Rome in 410, Jerome's retreat was disturbed by refugees from the city and raids by the Huns. He was also persecuted by the Pelagians, a heretical Christian sect, who assaulted his followers and set fire to the monas-

tery. His remains are said to have been taken to the church of
St Maria Maggiore in Rome in the thirteenth century. He is
usually represented with a lion, as he is said to have been on
friendly terms with one, from whose foot he removed a
thorn. His feast day is 30 September.

Joan of Arc [1412–1431]

St Joan was born in Domrémy, a village on the banks of the
Upper Meuse, on the borders of Lorraine. Her parents were
fairly well-off farmers, and she learned to sew and spin but
not to read or write. Throughout her childhood, France was
in a desperate state, racked by civil war between the dukes of
Burgundy and Orleans, and invaded by the English Henry V,
who overran Normandy and claimed the throne of France
from the mad Charles VI. After the murder of the duke of
Burgundy at the instruction of the dauphin, the Burgundians
allied themselves with the English. The dauphin, now
Charles VII, was meanwhile amusing himself at court. When
she was about thirteen, Joan heard voices telling her to be
good and to go often to church. She saw visions of St
CATHERINE and St MARGARET, whose appearance had been
foretold by St MICHAEL, who appeared in front of her with
angels. The voices soon gave more specific instructions:
Joan was to go to France, have the dauphin crowned at
Rheims and deliver France from her enemies. At first she resisted; then, in 1428, she went to the captain of the nearest
walled town, Vaucouleurs, told him of her mission and asked
to be led to the dauphin. He just laughed, and Joan returned
home. The next year, when she was seventeen, she tried
again. This time she was successful. An unexpected defeat,

which she had foretold, shook the captain out of his scepticism, and he sent her to Charles. She dressed in man's clothes as protection for the journey. In order to test Joan's supernatural powers, Charles had disguised himself, but she singled him out from his courtiers at once and, in private, finally convinced him by telling him personal matters that were so secret that they could only be known by divine revelation. Joan was then sent to Poitiers to be examined by a board of theologians who could find no faults. Joan's voices told her that she had just over a year to succeed in her mission, and she was frantic at the delays. At last she was accepted and given a household, a horse and armour. When she joined the troops, she had a banner with Christ crucified painted on it. She led the army from Blois, and when she entered Orleans two days later her courage revived the morale of the besieged city. The English forts were captured, and a week later Orleans was free. The relief of Orleans was followed by a week of victories and the surrender of Troyes. Charles VII was crowned at Rheims on 17 July 1429, with Joan standing beside him, holding her banner. He could probably have gone on to capture Paris, but Joan's advice was disregarded, and the attack when it did come was half-hearted—the king was not even present—and failed. In May 1430, Joan was taken prisoner at Compiègne by the Burgundians, abandoned by the king and sold to the English, who had always sworn to burn her if she ever fell into their hands. Cauchon, bishop of Beauvais, was the intermediary and bought her for the duke of Bedford for 10,000 livres. She was imprisoned in appalling conditions in the castle of Rouen, kept in irons in a damp cell with no privacy but instead the continual presence of rough English soldiers. She was half-starved and deprived of the Sacraments, but Charles made no attempt to intervene. In February 1431 her trial began, and she was charged with witchcraft and heresy. Her judges were ecclesiastical dignitaries, carefully chosen by Cauchon, her principal accuser, who hoped to curry favour with the English for preferment to the see of Rouen. Every attempt was made to make her deny the voices and confess that her supernatural powers came from the Devil. She defended herself with simplicity and intelligence, seldom allowing herself to be outwitted by the intricacies of theology. But then her voices stopped, and some sort of abjuration was wrung from her with the promise that she should be handed over to the Church to do lifelong penance in a convent and have the Sacraments restored to her. After three days, she revoked her abjuration. The voices had returned and told her that she was damning herself to save her life. She would not deny that she was sent by God, and any denial had been made through fear of the fire. She was then sentenced to be burnt, as having 'relapsed'. Before her death, on 30 May, she was given the Sacraments and then led to execution in the old marketplace of Rouen, beside the Church of St Saviour. On her head was put a paper mitre with the words 'Heretic. Relapsed. Apostate. Idolater' on it. There was a sermon, and her sentence was read out. St Joan then invoked the Trinity and the saints, singling some out by name. She asked for men's prayers, and forgave them the evil they had done her. After she had climbed onto the scaffold, she asked for a cross, and an English soldier made one out of two sticks and gave it to her. She also asked for one to be brought out from the church, and a Dominican friar held it up so that she could see it through the smoke. As she was swallowed up in the flames, she could be heard calling out the name of Jesus. Joan of Arc's ashes were thrown into the Seine. Twenty-three years later, at the insistence of her mother and brothers, her case was reopened, the tribunal's findings were quashed, and she was rehabilitated. Her feast day is 30 May.

John Chrysostom [died 407]

St John, called Chrysostom, or 'golden mouth', because of his eloquence, was born at Antioch. His father was commander of the Roman imperial troops and died when John was an infant. His mother, refusing all offers of marriage, devoted herself to his education. He was trained for the bar and attended the lectures of Libanius, the most famous orator of his day. John decided against practising law because it seemed to him inconsistent with the teachings of Christianity. He entered a religious community in the mountains south of Antioch. He spent four years there and two in a cave as a solitary, where he slept without lying down and endured extremes of cold and hunger, before his health broke down and he had to return to Antioch. He was ordained deacon in 381, and in 386 he was ordained priest by Bishop Flavian, who made him his preacher. From his ordination until his departure from Antioch in 397, his reputation as a preacher was enormous. The crowds that flocked to hear him were so great and so transfixed by his words that pickpockets found his sermons a golden opportunity and he had to warn his listeners to leave their purses at home. Towards the end of his ministry in Antioch, Emperor Theodosius I levied a new tax that caused the citizens to rise in revolt and destroy the statues of the emperor and his family. Then they were seized with terror at the consequences of their action. While they were in this state of penitence and suspense, John preached his most famous sermons, 'The Homilies on the Statues', and made many conversions. In 397 John left Antioch and became bishop of Constantinople, induced to do so by a stratagem. An imperial officer visited him in Antioch and invited him to visit the tombs of the martyrs outside the city. He was seized there and taken off to Constantinople by military escort. There he submitted to the inevitable and was consecrated bishop. At Constantinople, his preaching was as popular as ever, but he soon found himself in the middle of troubles. He set about a programme of reform, cutting down on expenses and giving the savings to the poor and to hospitals. His methods brought him into conflict with his clergy, wealthy lay Christians, and the Empress Eudoxia. He alluded to her in one sermon as Jezebel. His enemies succeeded in bringing about his banishment in 404, an event that nearly led to a popular uprising. Immediately afterwards, the city was shaken by an earthquake, and Eudoxia, in a panic, had him brought back. Soon John offended her again, and he was banished to Cucusus in Armenia, suffering great hardships on the journey. At Cucusus, his enemies arranged for him to be sent on to Pityus. He was so badly treated on the journey that he died of exhaustion in the chapel of St Basilicus. St John was the most prolific of all the saints, and his extant works fill thirteen volumes. He is often represented with a dove at his ear, or with the emblem of the beehive. His feast day is 13 September.

John of Damascus [*c*. 676–*c*. 754]
Also called **Joannes Damascenus** or **John Chrysorrhoas**
('the golden-flowing'), John of Damasus was a great theologian and hymn-writer of the Eastern Church. He was born in
Damascus to a Christian family known by the Arabic surname of Mansour. He was carefully educated, together with
his adopted brother, by the learned Italian monk Cosmas,
who had been brought to Damascus as a slave. He refuted the
iconoclastic measures of Leo the Isaurian with two memora-
ble addresses in which he vigorously defended the practice
of image-worship. It is said that Leo, unable to reach his for-
midable antagonist by open means, caused a treasonable letter to be forged as a result of which John's hand was struck
off by order of the khalif, but after a night of prayer to the
Virgin it was miraculously restored. It is certain that he spent
his later years in the monastery of St Sabas near Jerusalem,
where it is said he mortified his flesh with ascetic practices
of unusual severity. Here he found leisure and inspiration to
write his learned works and his religious poetry, was ordained a priest, and died. His feast day is 4 December.

John of God [1495–1550]
Born in Portugal, St John for forty years led an adventurous
life as a soldier and a keeper of Christian slaves among the
Moors. He then repented of his ways, his conversion being
so extreme that for a while he was locked up as a lunatic. In
1539 he pledged to devote himself to the sick and destitute,
earning his living as a wood merchant. Under the patronage
of the archbishop of Granada, he set up a house of shelter for
people in need, often being criticized for including prosti-

tutes and tramps. He died as a result of rescuing a man who was drowning in a flood. After his death, his followers were organized into the Brothers of St John of God—an order of hospitallers that spread far and wide. He is the patron saint of hospitals, nurses and the sick. His emblem is a pomegranate surmounted by a cross. His feast day is 8 March.

John of the Cross [1542–1591]

John was born in Avila, in Spain, to a noble family that had lost a great deal of its wealth. A Carmelite friar, he formed a friendship with St TERESA OF AVILA and in 1568 joined the first of the reformed houses of men of the order at Duruelo. He worked very hard to spread the reforms, and in 1577 was imprisoned at Toledo by order of the Carmelite prior general and was subjected to very brutal treatment. It was at this time that he started writing poetry. Escaping after nine months, he held various offices among the reformed friars and continued to write. But the order was racked with disagreeing factions. John supported the moderates, and he was removed from office and sent to a remote priory at La Peñuela. There he became ill and was moved to Ubeda, where he was again ill-treated and where he died. John's main works are *The Dark Night of the Soul*, *The Spiritual Canticle*, and *The Living Flame of Love*, with a second commentary on the first of these, *The Ascent of Mount Carmel*. In them, he wrote of his mystical experiences of religion with lyrical beauty. Because of his prolific writings, he is often depicted with many books. His feast day is 14 December.

John Ogilvie [1579–1615]

Born into a noble Scots family of mixed Presbyterian and

Catholic allegiance, John was the son of the head of the younger branch of the Ogilvies and of a daughter of Lady Douglas of Lochleven. When he was fifteen he was sent abroad to have a French Calvinist education but after a period of meditation and study he was received into the Catholic Church at the Scots college at Louvain. He trained as a Jesuit, making his vows as a member of the order in 1601. In 1610 he was ordained at Paris and then stationed at Rouen. Here he heard reports of the dire state of Catholicism in his home country and, after repeated requests, was sent to Scotland three years later. He was active in Edinburgh, Renfrew and Glasgow, before information from a pretended convert led to his arrest. He was put to the Scottish and French torture of 'the boot', and deprived of sleep for eight days and nights. But he refused, even at the entreaty of King James himself, to substitute crown for pope in temporal matters and would not divulge the names of other Scottish compatriots in religion. He was eventually hanged in Glasgow, having been found guilty of high treason. His feast day is 10 March.

John the Baptist [died *c*. 29]

John was said by Jesus to have been the greatest of all the prophets. He was the son of Elizabeth, cousin of the Virgin MARY, and Zachary, a temple priest, when they were in their old age—an event that had been predicted by an angel. In about the year 27, John began preaching in the wilderness of Judaea and baptising his followers, including Jesus himself, in the River Jordan. His message was that the people should repent because the kingdom of heaven was coming. John's public criticism of Herod Antipas for his incestuous mar-

riage to Herodias, his brother's wife, resulted in his imprisonment. He was executed without trial because of a trick—
when Salome, the daughter of Herodias, had delighted
Herod by her dancing, he agreed to grant her any wish she
wanted. At her mother's urging she insisted on receiving the
head of John the Baptist, which was duly brought in on a
plate. In the New Testament John hails Jesus as the lamb of
God. He himself is frequently depicted holding a lamb. His
feast day is 24 June.

John the Evangelist [first century]
Also called **John the Divine** (in the sense of theologian), St
John was the son of Zebedee and the brother of St JAMES THE
GREAT. With St PETER and St James, he belonged to the inner
circle of disciples and was present at the Transfiguration and
at Gethsemane during the Passion. With James, he asked Jesus to call down fire from heaven on the Samaritans who had
refused them shelter, and they went with their mother when
she asked Jesus if they could be placed on his right and left
hands in heaven. The brothers seem to have been full of zeal
but inclined to severity, and Jesus called them the 'Sons of
Thunder'. Universal tradition has identified St John as the
beloved disciple of the fourth Gospel—the disciple who sat
next to Jesus at the Last Supper and asked who would betray
him. John knew the high priest and gained admission into the
hall when Jesus was brought before Caiaphas. The author of
the Gospel according to St John, whether St John or not, had
certainly an inside view of the events that followed. It was to
John that Jesus commended his mother when the disciple
stood at the foot of the cross with Mary and the other

women. When the news of the Resurrection was brought to him by the women, he and Peter ran to the tomb and were the first to go inside. He was one of the seven disciples who went fishing on the Sea of Tiberias, and was the first to recognize Jesus standing on the shore. In the Acts of the Apostles, John was with St Peter when the lame man was healed at the Beautiful Gate of the Temple, and then went down to Samaria with him to lay hands on those that had been baptised. When St PAUL went to Jerusalem after his conversion, he was interrogated by John, with James and Peter. It is not clear when John left Jerusalem—probably after the martyrdom of St Peter and St Paul. He settled at Ephesus, but there is a tradition that he visited Rome and was thrown into a bath of boiling oil outside the Latin Gate, from which he miraculously escaped uninjured. This is celebrated on 6 May, the Festival of St John before the Latin Gate. According to Eusebius, bishop of Caesarea and author of a history of the Christian church, during the persecution of Domitian, John was condemned to exile on the island of Patmos, and it was here, towards the end of Domitian's reign, that he had his Revelation. After Domitian's death, John was free to return to Ephesus, and it is believed that he wrote his Gospel at that time. From Ephesus, he also governed the churches of Asia. He also wrote three epistles, one to all Christians, one to a local church, and one to Gaius, who had shown hospitality to visiting brethren. On a visit to a neighbouring city in Asia Minor, St John put a promising youth in the care of a new bishop. The youth was baptised but afterwards lapsed and became the leader of a band of robbers. When St John revisited the city, he insisted on tracking down the youth, being

taken prisoner by the robbers in the process. But he managed
to bring the youth back, repentant. At Ephesus, John opposed
the heretic, Cerinthus, and once refused to enter the baths
when he heard he was inside, fearing that the baths would
collapse because such an ungodly person was bathing there.
St John lived until he was about ninety-four, having, latterly,
to be carried into church to give his sermons. In his old age,
he is said to have kept a tame partridge. He died at Ephesus
in about the third year of Trajan's reign. He was the youngest
of the disciples, and the only one known positively not to
have been martyred. His feast day is 27 December.

Joseph
Husband of MARY THE BLESSED VIRGIN and foster father to Jesus, Joseph worked as a carpenter although he was descended from David, the king of the Jews. We know that the
family was poor because they could afford only one pair of
doves at Mary's purification in the temple. According to tradition he was a widower when he married Mary and died before Jesus began his ministry. It is stated emphatically that he
was a 'just' man, and the few biblical mentions of him give
an impression of a kind, dignified, self-effacing man. St
TERESA OF AVILA, among many others, assigned special value
to his intercession. His cult grew steadily, and in 1871 Pope
Pius IX proclaimed St Joseph patron of the whole Church.
He is represented with carpentry tools or a flowering rod or
wand. His feast days are 19 March and 1 May.

Joseph of Arimathaea [first century]
St Joseph was a wealthy Israelite, a good man who was seek-

ing the kingdom of God. He kept his allegiance to Jesus secret, for fear of the Jews. After the Crucifixion he overcame his fears and asked Pilate for Jesus' body, although by doing so he must have endangered his own life. With the help of Nicodemus, a Pharisee, the body was taken down and laid in Joseph's own tomb in a neighbouring garden, Nicodemus providing the spices and Joseph the fine linen. Joseph's authentic history ends with his involvement with Jesus' body, but legend associates him with Glastonbury. He is said to have been sent by PHILIP from Gaul (present-day France) to Britain in AD 63. Joseph landed with twelve monks and, although the king to whom they addressed themselves would not accept Christianity, he gave them an island, now known as Glastonbury Tor, on which they built a church of wattles. There Joseph stuck his thorn staff into the ground, where it took root and grew into a tree that flowered ever afterwards at Christmas. Later writers mention two silver containers that Joseph is said to have brought with him, one containing the blood and the other the sweat of Christ. He is often depicted with the emblems of the shroud, the crown of thorns, and nails. His feast day until 1969 was 17 March.

Jude [first century]

Also known as **Thaddaeus** and one of the twelve disciples, St Jude is traditionally identified with Jude, 'brother of James', the writer of the Epistle of Jude in the New Testament, but this is not certain. An apocryphal document alleges that Jude preached the gospel and was martyred in Persia with his fellow apostle SIMON. He was venerated in the Middle Ages but his cult later suffered as his name became confused with that of Judas Iscariot, the betrayer of Jesus Christ. Because of this resemblance, for centuries no one would invoke him for anything—hence his willingness to help people even in the most desperate situations, as the readers of personal columns in newspapers will be aware. His emblem is a club or a lance. His feast day (with SIMON) is 28 October.

Justin the Martyr [*c.* 100–*c.* 165]
Justin was a native of Flavia Neapolis, the ancient Sichem, in Samaria. His father, Priscus, was a heathen, and Justin was educated in the religion of his father. He became an ardent student of the philosohy of his time, beginning with the school of the Stoics but finally adhering to that of the Platonists. He ascribes his conversion to Christianity in one account to the firmness of the Christian martyrs, in another to a chance meeting with a holy stranger who directed him to study the Jewish prophets and the great Christian teacher whom they foretold. After his conversion he retained the garb of a philosopher, and appears to have wandered from place to place, as we find him disputing at Ephesus and Rome. His martyrdom is supposed to have taken place some time between 148 and 165, but the story rests on no sure historical evidence. He was one of the earliest and most distinguished apologists of the Christian church, and his works, although not very voluminous, are highly interesting and important. The only books ascribed to him with certainty are two, *Apologies for the Christians* and a *Dialogue with Trypho the Jew*. His feast day is 1 June.

K

Kentigern [died 612]

Also known as **Mungo**, St Kentigern was bishop of Glasgow, and the friend of St David and St Columba. He was said to have been the illegitimate son of a Pictish princess. For her sin against chastity his mother was condemned to be thrown from the top of a high hill, but she escaped miraculously without injury, only to be cast adrift in a coracle in the Firth of Forth. The coracle drifted across the estuary to Culross, where she was looked after by St **Serf**, the apostle of western Fife about whom little is known. When her son was born, the saint baptised mother and child and took them under his protection. The boy was christened Kentigern, but as he grew up Serf grew extremely fond of him, and he became known as Mungo, which means 'dear one' or 'darling'. Kentigern went to live in a cell near Glasgow, feeling himself called to a life of self-denial, but his fame spread and soon a community gathered around him, and he was consecrated bishop. It is said that he was driven into exile for a time in Wales, where he stayed with St David. When he returned to Glasgow, he laid the foundations of a cathedral on a burying ground consecrated by St Ninian. The present cathedral, which stands on the same site, is dedicated to St Kentigern. Followers of the saint carried his mission as far as

Galloway and Orkney, and St Columba came from Iona with a large company of monks to visit him. In the arms of the city of Glasgow, St Kentigern is represented with a fish and a ring. These come from the legend that said that King Roderick's queen gave a ring he had given her to her lover, a knight. The king saw it on the knight's finger and later pulled it off when the knight was sleeping and threw it into the River Clyde. He then went to the queen and challenged her to produce the ring. Being unable to do so, she was imprisoned and sentenced to death. She was allowed three days' grace, and she sent for Kentigern and begged for his help. Kentigern, remembering the troubles of his own mother, was filled with pity and prayed for her. Immediately afterwards the ring was found in a salmon that had been caught in the Clyde. It was brought to St Kentigern who sent it to the queen. She showed it to her husband and was pardoned. She then confessed to the saint and promised to do penance. Kentigern lived a most austere life. He recited the whole Psalter every day, often standing in the icy water of the Clyde, and slept with a stone for his pillow. His feast day is 13 January.

Keyne [c. 490]

This saint was a holy virgin whose name survives in an old church in Cornwall, near Liskeard, and still more so in its famous well. According to legend, whichever of a newly married couple drinks the water first will rule the roost. Her feast day is 8 October.

L

Lambert [died 709]

Lambert was born into a noble family in Maastricht and educated by the local bishop, Theodard. When the bishop was murdered in 670, Lambert succeeded him as bishop of the diocese of Tongres-Maastricht, which he ruled until the death of Childeric II caused him to be expelled from his see. For seven years Lambert stayed at the monastery of Stavelot, until the murder of Childeric's successor, Ebroin, restored him to his see. He set about the conversion of the pagans who lived among the sands and marshes of the Campine. He is said to have travelled as far as Frisia. St Lambert was murdered about 709. He was said to have been pierced by a javelin, from which his patronage of surgeons arose. He was buried at Maastricht and is venerated as a martyr. The occurrence of miracles caused the building of a church on the site of the house in Liège where he met his death. His feast day is 17 September.

Lawrence [died 258]

St Lawrence was archdeacon of Rome during the persecution of the Christians by Valerian. As keeper of the treasures of the church, he was ordered by the authorities to produce them. He asked for a day in which to collect them and spent

the time visiting the poorest parts of the city. The next day he
appeared at the tribunal, accompanied by a crowd of beggars
and cripples. 'These,' he explained, 'are the treasures of the
church.' He was ordered to be roasted on a gridiron but showed
no sign of suffering, and those who saw him said that his face
was like that of an angel. He spoke once to his executioners,
saying, 'Turn me, I am done on this side!' St AUGUSTINE
speaks highly of his qualities and the power of his intercession. His emblems are a book, a dish of coins and a gridiron,
and he is the patron saint of cooks. His feast day is 10 August.

Leonard [died *c*. 560]

St Leonard was a godson of Clovis I, king of the Franks. He
was a Frankish nobleman who was converted by St
REMIGIUS. He entered the religious life first in a monastery
and then as a hermit in a forest near Limoges, where he built
a cell. The king hunted in this forest, and when his wife was
in danger of dying in childbirth she was saved by the prayers
of St Leonard. In thanks, the king promised St Leonard as
much land as he could ride round in a night on a donkey. On
this land he founded a monastery, the abbey of Noblac,
where the town of Saint-Leonard was established later. St
Leonard is the patron saint of women in labour. It is said that
Clovis released every prisoner visited by the saint. He is
shown in art carrying fetters, and released prisoners would
hang up their manacles in churches dedicated to him. His
feast day is 6 November.

Louis [1215–1270]

St Louis IX became king of France at the age of twelve, and

seven years later married Margaret of Provence, elder sister of Eleanor, wife of Henry III of England. They had eleven children. He was brought up strictly by his mother, Blanche of Castile, who used to tell him that she would rather he were dead than that he should commit one mortal sin. Under her influence he developed the qualities that made him a saint. He was courageous, wise and magnanimous. He imposed a strict discipline on himself, hearing two Masses a day, fasting and wearing sackcloth next to his skin. He washed beggars' feet and ministered to lepers. He founded many religious houses and a hospital for the blind poor, and helped his friend and confessor Robert de Sorbon in the setting up of the theological college that grew into the Sorbonne. In gratitude to St Louis for his charity to the Christians in Palestine and other parts of the East, the Latin emperor at Constantinople presented him with the Crown of Thorns. To enshrine this, St Louis pulled down his own chapel of St Nicholas in the Ile de la Cité and built on its site the beautiful Sainte-Chapelle. The main work on Notre Dame de Paris was completed during his reign. In 1243 he had a serious illness from which he nearly died. As soon as he was able to speak he called for a crusader's cross and put it on, much to the dismay of his mother and the court. When he was well again, he set off on a crusade to the Holy Land to help recapture Jerusalem. He was gone for six years and proved himself to be a gallant soldier. He was immensely humble, and when his men were hit by a virulent illness, he superintended their burial, carrying putrid corpses himself 'without stopping his nostrils'. The crusaders were heavily defeated at Mansurah, and Louis was taken prisoner. After his release he withdrew the remnants of his troops to Akka in Palestine and from there to France. In 1270 he set off, against the advice of all his counsellors, on another crusade, but his army had only got as far as Tunis when he fell sick and died. His old servant summed up the character of the saintly king: 'He several times imperilled his life for the love he had for his people, when he could have done otherwise had he wished.' His emblems are a crown and sceptre, the regalia of royalty. His feast day is 25 August.

Lucian [c. 240–311]

St Lucian was born in Samosata in Syria, and studied rhetoric, philosophy and the Scriptures under Macarius, whose school of biblical criticism was famous. As well as his work as a priest, he revised the text of the Greek version of the Old Testament and that of the four Gospels. For a period of years he was separated from the Catholic communion. It is possible that he was suspected of following the heretic Paul of Samosata, but it is known that he died in communion with the church. During the persecution of Diocletian he was thrown into prison in Nicomedia and was tortured by having his legs dislocated at the hip and being left to starve to death. Fourteen days later, on Epiphany, he asked to receive the Eucharist and, being unable to sit or stand, used his breast as an altar. He died the next day. His feast day is 7 January.

Lucy [died c. 304]

St Lucy was the child of wealthy Christians in Syracuse in Sicily. Her father died when she was a child. St Lucy took an early, secret vow of perpetual virginity, but her mother was unaware of this and urged her to marry a pagan suitor. When Lucy confessed her vow, and her wish to enter the religious life, her mother offered no opposition, but the suitor, disappointed and angry, betrayed her to the governor as a Christian. St Lucy was condemned to work in a brothel, but the guards were unable to move her from where she stood. They then tried to burn her, without success, and at last she was put to death by having a sword thrust down her throat. St Lucy's name means 'light'. There are legends that her eyes were put out at the order of Diocletian, or that she tore them out herself when an admirer praised their beauty. Her feast day is 13 December.

Luke [first century]

St Luke was a Gentile, almost certainly a Greek, of Syrian Antioch, and a doctor. He was the author of the third Gospel, which is the fullest and most factual. From his Gospel we have the story of the Annunciation and of several miracles and parables not mentioned elsewhere. We know nothing about how he was converted, but he was probably a disciple of St PAUL. Paul refers to him as 'my beloved physician'. In the Acts of the Apostles, Luke follows the sequence of events after Jesus' Ascension. He dwells at length on the actions of St Paul, whom he accompanied from the start of his mission. Luke died, unmarried, in Greece at the age of eighty-four. There is a tradition that St Luke was a painter, which seems to be unfounded, and he is the patron saint of painters. His feast day is 18 October.

M

Machutus [died 627]

Machutus is also known as **Malo, Maclovius** and **Maclou**.
He was a Welshman, born at Caer-Gwent in Monmouthshire,
and educated at the monastery of Llancarfan. He wanted to
become a monk, but his parents did not approve, and he took
refuge for some time on an island in the Severn. Eventually
he was ordained priest and went to Brittany. St Machutus
was an evangelist who also built churches and founded monasteries. He became bishop of Aleth (Saint-Servan) and
made many converts, but the death of the chief who had been
his protector led to a change in his luck. He had to flee from
Aleth and sailed to Saintes. He was recalled after some years
to dispel a bad drought that was thought to be a punishment
for the sins of the people against their bishop. As Machutus
came off the ship, rain fell, but he did not stay long and died
on the voyage back to Saintes. He founded a monastery on
the island where St Malo now stands. His feast day is 15 November.

Madeleine Sophie [1779–1865]

St Madeleine Sophie Barat was born at Joigny. Her brother,
Louis, was a deacon and gave her a good grounding in the
liberal arts. She wanted to become a Carmelite lay sister, but

131

at the request of the superior of the Sacred Heart fathers, Joseph Varin, she went in 1801 to teach in a convent school in Amiens, where she became superior. This was the first house of the Society of the Sacred Heart, for the education of girls, which Mother Barat was to direct for sixty-three years, during which time it became established in twelve countries of Europe and America. She was canonized in 1925. Her feast day is 25 May.

Malachy [c. 1095–1148]
Malachy was born in Armagh and early in his career as a priest he inclined to the Roman system rather than the Celtic. In 1121 he became abbot of Bangor, and in 1125 was elected to the see of Connor. In 1132 he became archbishop of Armagh. Appointed papal legate for Ireland, he twice went to Rome, visiting St BERNARD at Clairvaux going and returning. In 1142 he founded the first Cistercian abbey in Ireland. On his return from Rome on his second journey, he stopped at Clairvaux where, on All Saint's Day 1148, he died of a fever in St Bernard's arms. He was canonized by Clement IV. The spurious 'Prophecies of St Malachy' were first published in 1595. They consist of Latin mottoes for the popes from 1143 onwards. His feast day is 3 November.

Malo *see* **Machutus**.

Margaret of Antioch
All that is known about Margaret is her legend, which travelled from Syria to Europe with the returning crusaders of the eleventh century. She is said to have been the daughter of a pagan priest of Antioch in Pisidia. She was brought up by a

Christian foster mother but when she returned to her father's
house, he sent her away when he learned that she had converted to the new religion. She went back to her foster
mother and earned her keep by looking after sheep. The prefect Olybius passed by and, being struck by her great beauty,
fell in love with her. He declared his intentions of marrying
her, or buying her if she was a slave. But Margaret said she
served only Jesus Christ. Having confessed that she was a
Christian, she was imprisoned and tortured. It is said that the
Devil appeared to her in the form of a dragon and disappeared when she held a cross up in front of him. After renewed torture, she was beheaded. Perhaps the chief interest
of her story is that JOAN OF ARC believed that she, with St
CATHERINE, appeared to her constantly and advised her in all
her attempts to save France. Her emblem is a dragon, which
she is often depicted as trampling underfoot. Her feast day
until 1969 was 20 July.

Margaret of Scotland [*c.* 1045–93]
Margaret was probably born in Hungary, the daughter of the
exiled Atheling Edward (son of Edmund Ironside, king of
England in 1016) and of Agatha, said to be a kinswoman of
Gisela, queen of St Stephen of Hungary and sister of the
Emperor Henry II. It is not certain when she came to England, or how long she had been there when, in 1068, with her
mother and sister (Christina) and her brother, Edgar the
Atheling, she fled from Norman England and was driven
ashore at the place now called St Margaret's Hope. Young,
lovely, learned and pious, she won the heart of the Scottish
king, Malcolm Canmore, who married her at Dunfermline.

She did much to civilize Scotland, and still more to assimilate the old Celtic church to the rest of Christendom on such points as the due beginning of Lent, the Easter communion, the observance of Sunday, and marriage within the prohibited degrees. She built a church at Dunfermline and established Benedictine monks there, and re-founded Iona. She bore her husband six sons and two daughters, and died three days after him in Edinburgh Castle. Pope Innocent IV canonized her in 1250. Her head, which had found its way from Dunfermline to Douai, was lost in the French Revolution; but her remaining relics are said to have been enshrined by Philip II in the Escorial. Her feast day is 16 November.

Mark [first century]

St Mark the Evangelist is generally believed to be John Mark, cousin of St BARNABAS and son of the Mary whose house was one of the meeting places of the brethren at Jerusalem. He was probably a Levite and a Cypriot. He is thought to have been the young man who followed Jesus after his arrest, and who ran away naked when he was caught, leaving his linen garment behind him. St Mark went with St PAUL and St Barnabas on their first missionary journey, but left them at Perga and returned to Jerusalem. Some scholars think that he disapproved of Paul's preaching to the Gentiles, others that he found the journey too dangerous. Paul found him unreliable and refused to take him on the mission to Cilicia and Asia Minor. Barnabas wanted to include Mark, and he fell out with Paul, sailing himself with Mark to Cyprus instead. Paul writes about Mark ten or twelve years later, referring to him as a fellow worker in Rome. It is a tradition that St Mark acted as an interpreter for St PETER at Rome. It was at Rome that Mark wrote the second Gospel, probably between AD 65 and 70, and is said to have been helped to compile it by Peter. Mark became bishop of the see of Alexandria. Later he was arrested for his faith, tortured by being dragged over stones and executed. His relics are believed to have been taken to Venice in the ninth century. His symbol is a lion, perhaps because of the medieval belief that lion cubs were born dead, being brought to life three days later by their fathers' roars (St Mark was considered to be the especially the historian of the Resurrection.) His feast day is 25 April.

Martin [died 401]

St Martin was born in Pannonia (now Hungary). His family were pagans, and his father, a soldier, wanted his son to follow in the same career and enrolled him in the army when he was fifteen. Martin disliked army life, and during his five years as a serving officer he lived in a very humble way, sharing his tent and his meals with his servant and helping him with his duties. One day, during a bitterly cold winter, Martin came across a beggar at the city gate in Amiens, shivering with cold. Martin had no money to give him, but he took off his cloak, cut it in half with his sword and gave half to the beggar. That night he dreamed of Jesus, surrounded by angels, wearing the half cloak. Martin was baptised, and asked for a discharge from the army, believing that as a Christian he was not allowed to fight. He was accused of cowardice, and his answer, according to legend, was to stand unarmed in the battle line holding only a cross, at the sight of which the enemy surrendered. Martin became a disciple of

St Hilary of Poitiers. He opposed the Arians in the Roman province of Illyricum with such force that he was publicly whipped and driven from the country. Hearing that the Church of Gaul (now France) was under Arian control and Hilary banished, he remained in Milan for some time. Driven from Milan by the Arian bishop, he took refuge on an island in the Gulf of Genoa, where he stayed until Hilary was recalled to his see. Hilary gave Martin a piece of land, and he lived there and attracted many disciples. This community grew into a great monastery, the first in Gaul, which was still there over fourteen centuries later. In 371 the people of Tours agitated for Martin to be made bishop. He was so reluctant that they had to trick him into visiting the house of a sick woman, where they took him prisoner and carried him off before the bishops. The bishops were not anxious to appoint Martin, partly because of his rough and unkempt appearance, but their objections were overruled by the clergy and the people, and he was consecrated. His diocese was mainly pagan, but soon his instruction and the example of his own life had an effect. He destroyed temples and idols and worked many miracles. On one occasion the priests agreed to fell their idol, a large fir tree, if Martin would stand directly in the path of its fall. The tree was cut and was about to fall on the bishop when he made the sign of the cross and it swerved and fell to one side. In order to avoid the crowds who sought him out, Martin retired to a cell on a steep cliff where he was joined by eighty disciples who shared his very austere life. This was the beginning of the abbey of Marmoutier. Martin had many visions. In one of these, the Devil appeared disguised as Christ in glory. But Martin looked in vain for the marks of the Passion and was not deceived. In 384, in Trèves, Priscillian and six companions who had been condemned for heresy, appeared before the Emperor Maximus. The bishops who had condemned them in the ecclesiastical court insisted on their execution. But St Martin protested against their being brought before the secular power at all and insisted that excommunication was a sufficient punishment. He refused to leave Trèves until the emperor promised to reprieve them. But no sooner had he gone than the bishops persuaded the emperor to break his promise and Priscillian and his followers were executed. This was the first occasion on which men were put to death for heresy by Christians. St Martin was furious and publicly excommunicated the bishops responsible, but later took them back into his communion in exchange for a pardon from Maximus for certain men condemned to death, and his promise to stop the persecution of the remaining followers of Priscillian. Martin was buried at Tours, and two thousand monks followed his body to the grave. It was said that the boat that carried his body floated upstream without oars or sail to the sound of heavenly music and that the trees on the banks burst into blossom. The oldest church in England is dedicated to St Martin. It stands outside the walls of Canterbury and was built, according to BEDE, during the Roman occupation. Its first dedication is unrecorded, but when Ethelbert offered it for the use of St AUGUSTINE it was known as St Martin's. His feast day is 11 November.

Mary Magdalene [first century]

Magdalene probably means 'of Magdala', a town near the

Sea of Galilee. Mary Magdalene was the woman from whom seven devils were cast out. She was one of a band of other women, healed of similar infirmities, who went with Jesus on some of his missionary travels and put their possessions at his disposal. She stood at the foot of the Cross with the Virgin MARY, Salome, Mary, the wife of Cleophas, and St JOHN THE EVANGELIST. After the Crucifixion Mary went to the tomb early, before dawn, and finding that the stone had been rolled away from the entrance ran to tell PETER and John. When they saw the empty tomb, Peter and John went back home, but Mary stayed there, weeping. When she looked into the empty tomb, she saw two angels in white, who asked her why she wept. Turning away, she saw Jesus standing before her but she did not recognize him, taking him to be one of the gardeners, until he said, 'Mary,' to her. She went, as he told her to, and told the disciples what had happened. It is believed in the Greek church that Mary Magdalene followed John to Ephesus, and died and was buried there. The widespread tradition that identifies her with the unnamed repentant prostitute who anointed Jesus' feet with ointment from an alabaster box has been repudiated by the Church. Its widespread currency in the Middle Ages, however, made Mary Magdalene the patron saint of penitent sinners and repentant prostitutes. Her feast day is 22 July.

Mary the Blessed Virgin

Little is known of Mary, the mother of Jesus. St LUKE tells the story of the Annunciation by the angel, the birth at Bethlehem and the Purification. On the Cross, Jesus put her into the care of St JOHN, saying to him, 'Behold thy mother.' She is not mentioned as having seen Jesus after the Resurrection, but the tradition is that he appeared to her first. In the Acts of the Apostles she is mentioned as continuing to pray with the disciples. One tradition says that she died in Jerusalem; another that she went with John to Ephesus and was buried there. The site of the tomb of the Virgin, to the north of the garden of Gethsemane, is not mentioned by any traveller of the first six centuries. The feast of the Assumption, on 15 August, is the traditional date of her death, and there is a legend that when the Apostles opened her tomb they found that there was no body, but it was full of lilies and roses. This story is of late date and probably arose to account for the popular belief that her body was taken up into heaven. She has many emblems, including the unicorn, the lily and a spring of running water. Her principal feast day is 15 August.

Matthew [first century]

St Matthew was a Jew, probably a Galilean. As a publican, a tax gatherer for the Romans, he was barred from communion in the religious worship of the Jews and was disliked by Jew and Gentile alike. The name Matthew means 'gift of Jehovah', and was probably given to him after he was called to follow Jesus. This call is recorded in his Gospel and tells how Jesus came up to him while he sat at his table collecting taxes and said, 'Follow me.' Matthew celebrated his call by giving a feast at which Jesus was present, to the horror of the Pharisees, who objected to him eating with publicans and sinners. He is said to have preached in Ethiopia, and to have been the guest at one time of the eunuch of Queen Candace, and to have been killed with a sword (he may have this as an

emblem), but other records report that he died a natural
death. His feast day is 21 September.

Matthias [first century]

After the death of Judas, St Peter ordained that it was necessary to elect a twelfth Apostle. Two candidates were chosen
from among the seventy-two disciples 'which have been with
us all the time that the Lord Jesus went in and out among us'.
Both were qualified to bear witness to the life of Jesus so the
decision was made by drawing lots, and Matthias was chosen. One tradition says that he preached in Ethiopia and was
martyred there, another that he stayed in Jerusalem and, having converted many with his preaching, was accused of
Christianity. When the judge wanted to give him time to
think about renouncing his faith, Matthias said, 'God forbid
that I should repent of the truth that I have truly found.' He
was taken away, stoned and beheaded. His body is said to
have remained in Jerusalem for a long time and then to have
been taken to Rome by St HELENA, the mother of Constantine
the Great. St Matthias is represented in art carrying an axe,
and sometimes a book and a stone. His feast day is 14 May.

Methodius *see* **Cyril** and **Methodius**.

Michael

One of the three angels who stand before the throne of God,
St Michael is described in the Book of Revelations as the
leader of the heavenly armies in their battle against the Devil
and his forces. He is the protector of Christians in general
and soldiers in particular, and was considered in the East to
be the special guardian of the sick. Outside Constantinople

there was a church bearing his name from the time of
Constantine. Michael is the angel who receives risen souls
and weighs them in the balance—the basis of his patronage
of grocers. Many visions of him have been seen, and an appearance in the eighth century led to the foundation of Mont-
Saint-Michel Abbey in Normandy. His feast day is 29 September.

Monica [died 388]
St Monica is best known as the mother of St AUGUSTINE, the
bishop of Hippo. She was born in North Africa to Christian
parents who, as soon as she was old enough to marry, found
her a husband, Patricius, who was extremely bad-tempered
and unfaithful. She also had to share her home with an un-
sympathetic mother-in-law and, in desperation, took to alco-
hol. She overcame this addiction, and by her patience and
good nature converted Patricius to Christianity. He was baptised a year before his death. Her sweet nature also won over
her mother-in-law. St Monica then tried to convert Augustine, who was at this time leading a life of debauchery and
self-indulgence. To escape her constant pleas, Augustine
went to Italy in 383, but Monica followed him, first to Rome
and then to Milan. Here, with the help of St AMBROSE, Augustine accepted the Christian faith in 386 and was baptised the
following year. Monica is said to have declared that all her
hopes had now been fulfilled and that she had no more need
of an earthly life. Soon afterwards, as she and her son were
on their way back to Africa, she died in Ostia, in Italy. Her
feast day is 27 August.

Mungo *see* **Kentigern**.

N

Nicholas [died *c*. 326]

St Nicholas, also known as Santa Claus, is one of the most popular of all the saints. He was bishop of Myra (now Mugla in southwest Turkey) during the fourth century. A church was dedicated to him by Roman Emperor Justinian about 560, and since the tenth century he has been known and revered in the West. He was born at Patara, in Asia Minor, and on the day of his birth is said to have stood up in his bath and praised God. As a very young child he insisted on fasting on Wednesdays and Fridays, and he began to study theology at the age of five. He grew up a rich man and spent his money on helping the poor. He once heard that a nobleman who had lost his money was about to turn his three daughters out on to the streets, as he could not afford dowries for them. On three successive nights Nicholas threw a bag of gold through the nobleman's window, saving the girls from a life of prostitution. From this act comes his symbol of three golden balls, since adopted by pawnbrokers. On a voyage to the Holy Land he saved the ship from being wrecked by his prayers, and thus became the patron saint of sailors. He is also the patron saint of children. St Nicholas is said to have saved his city from famine by persuading the captains of some ships carrying corn, which stopped at Myra on their way to Alexandria, to unload part of their cargo. He promised that when they got to Alexandria nothing would be missing, and they found this to be true. He is said to have died and been buried in Myra, but his relics were taken to Bari in Italy in 1084. The custom of giving presents in his name originated among the Protestant Dutch. Other symbols of Nicholas apart from the three golden balls are three purses, three children in a tub, and an anchor. His feast day is 6 December.

Ninian [c. 360–c. 432]
Also called **Ringan**, Ninian was born of noble parents in Galloway in southern Scotland on the shores of the Solway Firth. Studious and ascetic, he made a pilgrimage to Rome, and there, after some years' stay, he was consecrated bishop by the pope. On his way home to become the first known apostle of Scotland, he visited St MARTIN at Tours, and after his arrival at Galloway he founded the 'Candida Casa,' or church of Whithorn, dedicating it to St Martin, the news of whose death had just reached him. Later he worked successfully for the evangelization of the Southern Picts, and died in 432 (according to one tradition) 'perfect in life and full of years,' and was buried in his church at Whithorn. His feast day is 26 August.

O

Olaf [995–1030]

The half-brother of Harald III of Norway, at the age of twelve he became a Viking mercenary. He made several attacks on Frisia, Normandy, Spain and England, including an attack on London that culminated in London Bridge being pulled down by grappling irons. In 1013 he was converted to Christianity and in 1015 succeeded in wresting the throne of Norway from Erik and Svend Jarl. The severity with which he endeavoured to exterminate paganism by fire and sword alienated his subjects, who rebelled against him when Cnut of Denmark invaded Norway in 1028. Olaf fled to the court of his brother-in-law, Jaroslav of Russia, who gave him a band of 4000 men with whom he returned in 1030 in an attempt to regain the throne. Olaf and Cnut met in battle at Stiklestad, where Olaf was defeated and slain. His body was taken to the cathedral of Trondhiem from where the fame of its miraculous power spread far and wide; and Olaf was solemnly proclaimed patron saint of Norway in the succeeding century. His feast day is 29 July.

Oswald [died 642]

Oswald was the first of the English royal saints. He belonged to the royal family of Bernicia, and when excluded from the

144

throne during the reign of Edwin, whose kingdom of Northumbria included Bernicia, took refuge among the Scots and
was converted by them to Christianity. He distinguished
himself as a Christian soldier by defeating Cadwalader at the
battle of Heavenfield in 635, after Edwin and his sons had
been killed and their country ravaged by the heathen prince.
Before the battle he erected a cross and called his army to
kneel and pray in front of it. After his victory, Oswald asked
the Scottish elders who had baptised him to send him a
bishop to establish the Christian faith in his kingdom. In response they sent him AIDAN, and Oswald appointed the island of Lindisfarne as his see. BEDE tells how Oswald listened humbly to Aidan's advice and set about extending the
Church throughout his kingdom. In the early days of Aidan's
ministry, before he could speak English fluently, the king
himself would translate for him as he preached. Priests and
monks flocked over the border into Britain, while the king
gave money and land to establish monasteries. Gradually the
kingdom and provinces of Britain were united under
Oswald's rule. Humble, kind and generous, the king often
prayed from the hour of the midnight office until morning.
He sat with his hands turned upwards on his knees, an atti-
tude he had adopted from constant prayer. One Easter, as
Oswald sat down to dine with Aidan, the king's almoner announced the arrival of a number of beggars asking for alms.
The king at once ordered his own food to be distributed, and
the silver dish broken in pieces and divided among them.
Aidan took hold of the king's right hand and said, 'May this
hand never perish.' The hand was said by Bede to be still un-
perished in the twelfth century. Oswald was killed at the Bat-

tle of Maserfield in the ninth year of his reign while fighting
against the heathen king of Mercia, and his last words were a
prayer for the souls of his soldiers, which became a proverb:
'O God, be merciful to their souls, as said Oswald as he fell.'
He was dismembered and his head and limbs nailed to a tree.
'Oswald's tree' may be the derivation of the Oswestry of to-
day. Oswald was succeeded by his brother Oswin, who removed the saint's head for burial at Lindisfarne and the arms
and body at Bamburgh. His feast day is 9 August.

P

Pancras [died 304]

St Pancras was a Phrygian of noble birth who was brought to
Rome on the death of his father by his uncle Dionysius. They
were both baptised by the pope and were martyred by
Diocletian soon afterwards. St Pancras was only fourteen
when he was beheaded. He is said to be the special enemy of
those who swear falsely. According to GREGORY OF TOURS, 'If
there be a man that will make a false oath in the place of his
sepulchre, he shall be travailed with an evil spirit or out of
his mind or he shall fall on the pavement all dead.' His feast
day is 12 May.

Patrick [died 463]

St Patrick was probably born near Dumbarton, on the River
Clyde in Scotland. His parents seem to have been of
Romano-British extraction, and his father was a deacon, also
working as a town councillor under the Roman government.
When he was fifteen, Patrick was carried off to slavery in
pagan Ireland by pirates. For six years he looked after pigs in
Armagh. During this time he had a great spiritual awakening,
felt 'the Spirit burning within him,' and dedicated his life to
God. After seven years he escaped and went home, but in his

147

dreams the Irish called to him to return and, in spite of the entreaties of his family, he decided to return as a missionary. He seems to have gone back as a layman and, after preaching for some time, to have visited Gaul (now France) and Italy, and to have studied under St GERMAN at Auxerre. It seems probable that it was German who consecrated Patrick bishop and sent him to Britain to replace Palladius, who had died among the Picts less than a year after the beginning of his mission. Patrick was over sixty when he returned to Ireland and began to preach in the country where he had once been a slave. He began his work in Ulster and then attempted the conversion of the high-king, Laoghaire, whose court was at Tara. It was here that Patrick came into direct conflict with the wizards, or Druids. He lit his pascal fire at Easter, which coincided with the Feast of Tara, when it was proclaimed that no fire should be lit before the fire of Tara, the penalty for disobedience being death. Patrick's fire lit up the whole area, and the wizards said that unless it was put out that same night it would burn until Doomsday. The king set out with chariots, meaning to kill Patrick. There is no record of their conversation, but his fire burned on, and the teaching of Christianity was tolerated after this. St Patrick travelled up and down Ireland, preaching, building churches and working miracles. He met with much opposition. One Ulster chief said of him, 'This is the shaven head and the falsifier who is deceiving everyone. Let us go and attack him, and see if God will help him.' But Patrick's courage never failed. The saint must have been an old man when he carried out his forty days' fast on Cruachan Aigli in Mayo, from which the Croagh Patrick pilgrimage is derived. The only contemporary evi-

dence of his life is found in his own writings, especially the
Confession, in which he reviews his life and work. What
stands out is his determination and modesty. He writes, 'I,
Patrick, a sinner, am the most ignorant and of least account
among the faithful, despised by many.' He wished to die in
Armagh, but an angel warned him that this must not be. It is
probable that he died in Saul on Strangford Lough, where he
built his first church. He had a worthy funeral and was
'waked' for twelve nights. After his death many legends
grew up around St Patrick. One was that he explained the
Trinity by reference to the shamrock, another that he expelled all snakes from Ireland. As a result his emblems are
shamrocks and snakes. His feast day is 17 March.

Paul [died 67]

St Paul was the Apostle chosen by God to preach the Gospel
to the Gentiles and make Christianity a world religion. He
was born at Tarsus and enjoyed the privileges of Roman citizenship. His father was of the tribe of Benjamin, rich and of
some position. Saul, as his name was then, was educated
partly at Tarsus, where he learnt the trade of tent-making,
and was later sent to Jerusalem to study under the Pharisee
Gamaliel. He grew up a zealous adherent of Jewish law and
traditions, and threw himself with enthusiasm into the conflict with St STEPHEN and the followers of Jesus. He assisted
passively in the murder of Stephen by holding the cloaks of
those who were stoning the saint. Later he applied for a com-
mission to arrest all the Jews in Damascus who followed Jesus and to bring them as prisoners to Jerusalem. But on his
way, Jesus appeared to him saying, 'Saul, Saul, why persecu-

test thou me?' Trembling on the ground, Saul said, 'Lord, what wilt thou have me do?' Those travelling with Saul heard the voice but saw nothing, and when Saul rose from the ground he was blind and had to be led to Damascus. He stayed there for three days, fasting, until a disciple called Ananias came, laid his hands on him, and restored his sight. From being a persecuting Jew, Saul became a devout and enthusiastic follower of Jesus. He was baptised and began to preach Christianity in the synagogues. The local Jews saw him as a serious threat and planned to kill him, so he had to flee to Jerusalem. His life was in danger again there, and he was sent to Tarsus where he stayed for seven or eight years. In 44 St BARNABAS came to Tarsus, and the following year the two saints set off on their first missionary journey. In this work, Saul showed himself to be a genius as well as a saint. His plan was to make use of the Roman imperial administration by establishing the church strongly in the centres of the different provinces he visited so that it could spread out to the smaller towns and villages. Antioch, the centre of the southern part of Galicia, was the first in which he founded the church. It was followed by Thessalonica and Phillippi in Macedonia, at Corinth in Achaia, and at Ephesus in Asia, He then saw that he must do the same in Rome itself. This demanded courage, determination , energy and complete dedication. He had to face the opposition of the heathen, and of the Jews, who were even more bitterly opposed. The Apostle to the Gentiles is referred to as Saul in the earlier chapters of the Acts of the Apostles, and later as Paul. His Roman citizenship secured him a safe passage to Caesarea and a fair trial before King Agrippa when the Jews would have torn him to pieces in Jerusalem after his appearance in the temple. In Rome he was imprisoned for two years in a house he had rented, chained to a guard. There he wrote the Epistles to the Ephesians, Philippians and Colossians. He was acquitted and released in 62. There is no record of how he spent the next few years, but it seems certain that he revisited the churches he had founded in the East and probable that he preached in Spain. The only record of his second imprisonment is in his Second Epistle to Timothy, in which he urges him to visit him before winter, bringing his cloak, which he had left behind in Troy, and his books. Everyone had deserted him, apart from St LUKE, his 'beloved physician'. He wrote, 'I am now ready to be offered. I have finished my course, I have kept the faith.' He was beheaded in Rome. In an apocryphal work from the first century, there is a description of St Paul on a journey as a short man with a bald or shaven head, hollow-eyed and with a crooked nose. 'Sometimes he looked like a man. sometimes he had the appearance of an angel.' His emblems are a sword, book and scroll. His feast day is 29 June.

Paulinus of York [died 644]

Paulinus was described by BEDE as a man 'beloved of God'. He was consecrated bishop so that he could accompany Princess Ethelburga, daughter of Ethelbert, the Christian king of Kent, when she set off to marry Edwin, the pagan king of Northumbria. He was to say Mass for her every day and preserve her from being corrupted by the heathens. He was consecrated bishop by Archbishop Justus in 625. As soon as he entered the province, Paulinus set out to convert the king, who hesitated for a long time. Paulinus then reminded him of a promise the king had made in his youth—as an exile without friends he had been accosted by a stranger who had promised him more power than any English king had yet known, as long as he followed the good advice of someone who would follow after him. Edwin had given his word, and the stranger had laid his hand on his head, saying that would be the sign, before he vanished into mid air. When Paulinus repeated this and put his hand on Edwin's head, he called a council and asked their opinion of the new faith. The high priest, Coifi, was in favour of giving it a trial. Another priest agreed, comparing the life of man to the flight of a sparrow through the open doors of a banqueting hall. While he is inside he is safe from the winter storms, but after a few moments of comfort he vanishes again into the darkness which he came from. Similarly, man has a little time on this earth, and knows nothing of what went before or what follows. If the new religion could reveal new knowledge, they should certainly follow it. The others agreed, and Coifi led an attack on the heathen temple and destroyed its altars. King Edwin was baptised at York with the chief men of his kingdom. Conversions followed rapidly. At a pool near Hepple, in Northumberland, called Holywell ever since, St Paulinus is said to have baptised thirty thousand people in one day. Bede tells us that St Paulinus was 'a tall man, stooping a little, with black hair, thin face, and narrow, aquiline nose, venerable and awe-inspiring in appearance.' During the last years of Edwin's reign there was such peace and order that a proverb said 'a woman could carry her newborn baby across the island from sea to sea and suffer no harm.' But after six years of success, Paulinus' ministry in Northumbria came to an end. In 633 Edwin was killed in battle at Heathfield by Penda of Mercia and Cadwalader of Wales. The kingdom was in confusion, and Paulinus took the widowed Ethelburga and her children back to Kent by the sea route, leaving his deacon to do what he could for his scattered flock. In the same year he was appointed to the see of Rochester, where he remained until his death. His feast day is 10 October.

Perpetua [died 203]

Perpetua was one of a group of early Christian martyrs whose heroic deaths at Carthage in North Africa were recorded by their contemporaries. She was the daughter of a pagan Roman father and a Christian mother. She was twenty-two and the mother of a young baby when she died. Perpetua left behind her a record of her imprisonment and the trial of herself and her companions. This account takes us up to the day before the public games at Carthage, at which the condemned would be thrown to the wild beasts, and ends with the words, 'Of what was done in the games themselves, let him write who will.' The saint wrote without a trace of pity about the sufferings of the Christians in the dark and almost airless dungeon. To the very end, her father pleaded with her to renounce her faith and save herself. She refused to do this, although she was tortured by anxiety about her baby, from whom she was separated. Then she was allowed to have him with her, and wrote, 'I at once recovered my health, and my prison suddenly became a palace to me and I would rather have been there than anywhere else.' In prison Perpetua had a vision. She saw a golden ladder leading up to

heaven. It was very narrow, with swords, hooks and daggers
tied on to its sides and a dragon at the bottom. Saturnus (their
leader, who had not been arrested but had chosen to suffer
with them rather than desert them) climbed up first and
called down to Perpetua to follow. Using the dragon's head
as a step, she climbed up and found herself in a garden full of
people dressed in white. A tall shepherd turned to her and
said, 'Welcome, child.' From this vision, the martyrs understood that their time on earth was coming to an end. Perpetua
approached her death in a state of ecstasy. While the men
were mauled by leopards, boars and bears, Perpetua and the
other female martyr, **Felicitas**, were attacked by a mad cow
before being finally killed by the gladiators' swords. Their
feast day is 7 March.

Peter [first century]
St Peter was Jesus' most prominent disciple and became the
leader of the Apostles after his death. He was a Galilean of
Bethsaida and a fisherman, sharing his boat with his brother
Andrew, and James and John, the sons of Zebedee. Peter was
married, and in later life was accompanied by his wife on
some of his missionary journeys. He was introduced to Jesus
by his brother Andrew as Simon, and Jesus gave him the ad-
ditional name of Kephas, the Hebrew for 'rock', 'Petros', or
Peter, being the Greek equivalent. Throughout the Gospel
story, Peter stands out as a leading figure, divinely inspired
sometimes, but sometimes liable to act on impulse. Jesus,
who could foresee that Peter would deny him before the
servants of the High Priest, could still say to him, 'Thou art
Peter, and on this rock I will build my Church; and the gates

of Hell shall not prevail against it.' After the Ascension Peter
was prominent in the councils of the Apostles and in building
the growing church. The first miracle of healing recorded in
the Christian church was performed by Peter, who cured a
lame beggar when he asked for alms as Peter passed him on
his way into the temple. The persecution of the church at Jerusalem, following the martyrdom of St STEPHEN, scattered
its members throughout Judaea and Samaria, but Peter
stayed in Jerusalem. Later he went on missionary journeys to
Syria. At Joppa he saw a vision of a sheet let down from
heaven, containing all kinds of animals and birds. He heard a
voice saying, 'Arise, Peter; slay and eat. What God has
cleansed, that call thou not common.' Peter took this to be
authority for the admission of Gentiles to the church. Peter is
said to have been the first bishop of Syrian Antioch, occupy-
ing the see for two years or more. During the persecution of
Herod Agrippa I he was imprisoned but was released by an
angel although he was sleeping in chains between two soldiers. It is probable that Peter went to Rome during St PAUL's
first imprisonment and that he acted as bishop of the church
at Rome after Paul's release. In Samaria the Apostles met
Simon Magus, the sorcerer, who asked for the power the
Apostles had been given by Jesus. Peter told him to 'Keep
thy money to thyself,' because God's gift could not be
bought. There is a legend that Peter, with St Paul, met the
sorcerer again in Rome, where he was demonstrating his
magic to the Emperor Nero. Simon Magus climbed to the top
of a high tower, where he was crowned with a laurel wreath.
He announced that the Galileans had angered him and that he
would show that he could ascend to heaven himself. Then he

threw himself off the tower and began to fly about. Nero said to the two Apostles, 'This man is good—and you two are traitors.' Peter then called on the devils holding the sorcerer up to leave him, in the name of Jesus, and Simon Magus fell at once to the ground and broke his neck. Another legend says that on the night before St Peter's martyrdom he was persuaded to escape. But at the gate of Rome he met Jesus coming in, and when he asked him where he was going, Jesus replied, 'I am going to be crucified a second time.' Peter was overcome with shame and went back to Rome and met his death. He is said to have been crucified with his head downwards at his own request: 'I am not worthy to be put on the cross as my Lord was.' His body is believed to have been buried in the Vatican, near the Triumphal way, and to have been moved later to the cemetery on the Appian Way. Pope Cornelius is said to have restored it to the Vatican. It now rests in the great Church of St Peter. His emblem is an upturned cross. His feast day is 29 June.

Philip [first century]

St Philip was the first of the Apostles whom Jesus called to follow him. He came from Bethsaida and, according to Clement of Alexandria, it was generally accepted that he was the one who asked Jesus if, before going with him, he could first go and bury his father. Jesus replied, 'Let the dead bury their dead.' It was St Philip whom Jesus asked 'Whence shall we buy bread that these may eat?' and who answered, 'Two hundred pennyworth of bread is not sufficient.' His answer seems to show that he had calculated the amount required to feed the five thousand, without allowing for a miracle. The most persistent tradition says that St Philip carried the Gospel into Scythia and Phrygia. He preached in Asia for many years, baptising many people and ordaining priests and deacons. He is said to have been helped in his work by his two virgin daughters, and another who was buried at Ephesus. Like PETER, St Philip was crucified upside down. His feast day is 3 May.

Philip Neri [1515–1595]

Philip Neri was born in Florence. Although his uncle wished to make him his heir, he abandoned all worldly pursuits, left his family and took himself to Rome in his eighteenth year. There he spent most of his time visiting the sick, instructing the poor and ignorant, and in solitary prayer in the catacombs, where suddenly one day he felt strange heart palpitations and fracture of the ribs, which he attributed to the supernatural effects of divine love. In 1551 he became a priest and took up quarters in a little church, where he gathered round him a number of disciples and began the devotional exercises that made his name famous. These daily services, which were a great novelty, consisted of three sermons of about half an hour's duration, delivered in a familiar style and interspersed with vernacular hymns, reading, and prayers. His object was to make religion attractive, especially to the young. During carnival or in holiday seasons he instituted musical entertainments and religious dramas. At other times he took a procession through the streets on a pilgrimage to seven churches, alternating hymns and silent prayer. In 1574 an oratory, or mission hall, was built for him in Rome. Some of his companions had been ordained as priests, and he established them here as a community. Ten years later the community moved to Vallicella, where the institute of the Oratory received the formal approval of the pope, and here Philip died. He was canonized in 1622. His feast day is 26 May.

Pius V [1504–1572]

Born Michele Ghislieri, of poor parents in the village of Bosco, near Alessandria in Italy, at the age of fourteen he entered the Dominican order. His merit was recognized by Pope Paul IV, who named him bishop of Sutri and Nepi in 1556 and cardinal the following year. His austere temper led him, as inquisitor-general for Lombardy, to employ rigorous measures for repressing the Reformed doctrines. Under Pius IV he was translated to the see of Mondovi, and was chosen unanimously as his successor in 1566. As pope he worked to restore discipline and morality in Rome, reduced the expenditure of his court, prohibited bullfights and other amusements, suppressed prostitution, and regulated the taverns of the city. He zealously maintained the Inquisition and strove to enforce the disciplinary decrees of the Council of Trent. In 1568 he ordered the yearly publication of the celebrated bull, *In Coena Domini*—an attempt to apply to the sixteenth century the principles and legislation of GREGORY VII. and in 1570 excommunicated Elizabeth I of England. The most momentous event of his pontificate was the expedition that he organized, with Spain and Venice (the Holy League), against the Turks and that resulted in a decisive naval engagement in the Gulf of Lepanto in western Greece on 7 October 1571, when the Turks were defeated and their invasion of Europe prevented. Pius died in the following year and was canonized by Clement XI in 1712. His feast day is 30 April.

Pius X [1835–1914]

Born Giuseppe Sarto to humble parents at Riese near Venice, he studied at Treviso and Padua and was ordained priest in 1858. Soon he became chancellor of the diocese and vicar of the chapter of Treviso. Made bishop of Mantua in 1884 by Leo XIII and in 1893 cardinal and patriarch of Venice, he endeared himself by the simplicity of his life, his repression of abuses and sympathy with the poor. In August 1903 he was elected pope. Remarkable for piety and administrative activity rather than for learning, he was conservative in theology. He began a new codification of canon law and reformed the liturgy, but he insisted that church music should return from a florid and secular style to the sacred traditions of plainsong and that church choirs should not include women. In France and Portugal complete separation of church and state, and in Spain growing toleration, led to strained relations and embarrassment. Modernism in every shape was prohibited, and efforts to find a *via media* between the church and modern life brought to a standstill. His feast day his 21 August.

Polycarp [died *c*. 155]

Polycarp was one of a group of early bishops who were the immediate disciples of the Apostles. He himself was established by St JOHN as bishop of Smyrna in 96. Smyrna was the only church mentioned as being without blame. Obstinate and conservative, he is said to have stated that he would rather stop his ears than hear and argue against heretical doctrines. Because of this reputation, he is invoked against earache. When the heretic Marcion met Polycarp in the streets of Rome and asked him, 'Do you recognize me?' Polycarp replied, 'I recognize thee as the first-born of Satan.' As St IGNATIUS passed through Smyrna on his way to martyrdom St Polycarp kissed his chains. Ignatius told him to look after the church in Antioch and asked him to write to the churches in Asia to which he would not have time to write himself. The letter that Polycarp wrote to the Phillipians still exists. Towards the end of his life Polycarp visited Rome to confer with Bishop Anicetus about the date on which Easter should be kept. Neither could persuade the other to change his custom, but they each agreed to follow their own inclination and did not fall out. Anicetus showed his respect for his visitor by letting him celebrate Mass in his church. Persecution broke out in Asia in the sixth year of Marcus Aurelius. Polycarp waited calmly for his martyrdom, only changing his lodging. His whereabouts were betrayed by a slave who was threatened with torture, and his house was surrounded by horsemen. Polycarp refused to escape, saying, 'God's will be done.' He met his persecutors at the door and ordered supper for them, only asking for some time for prayer before he left. He prayed standing for two hours. He was urged by the proconsul to recant, but he refused. When the threat of being thrown to wild beasts failed to make him change his mind, he was threatened with fire. 'You threaten fire that burns but for a moment, for you know nothing of the judgement to come and the fire of eternal punishment,' he replied, adding, 'Bring what you will.' His hands were bound, and he was led to the stake. The bystanders were struck with the difficulty he had in taking off his boots, because for many years this had been done for him by a disciple. The pile was set alight but according to a letter written in the name of the church of Smyrna, the flames billowed out like the sails of a ship, gently encircling the body of the martyr, which remained in the middle, unburnt. There was a smell of incense. Polycarp was then pierced with a spear; a dove flew out, and enough blood flowed out to put out the fire. His feast day is 23 February.

Prisca [died 265]

Also known as **Priscilla**, very little is known about this saint except that she was revered as a martyr in Rome at a very early date and she is buried in the catacomb of St Priscilla. She was a Roman girl of consular rank who was accused of practising Christianity. The Emperor Claudius ordered her to sacrifice to idols, but she refused and was beaten and imprisoned. During the night she sang praises to God and had a vision of angels. The next day she was beaten again, but still refused. She was thrown to a lion, but the lion lay down at her feet and licked them. She was tortured by having her flesh torn by hooks and pincers and later, still refusing to give up her faith, she was taken outside the city and beheaded. She was thirteen years old. An eagle is said to have defended her body from dogs until it was collected by her fellow Christians. Her feast day is 18 January.

R

Remigius [died 530]

St Remigius was born at Laon, the child of noble Gaulish parents. When he was twenty-two the clergy and lay people of Rheims met in the cathedral to elect a bishop. A ray of sun shone in and lit up Remigius' face, and the congregation took this as a sign from heaven and made him their bishop, even although he was a layman. He occupied the see for over seventy years. He became famous throughout the church for his outstanding holiness, ability and eloquence. He set about converting the Franks to Christianity. The pagan Clovis, king of northern Gaul, had married a Christian princess, Chlotildis, daughter of the Burgundian king, Chilperic. Her efforts to convert her husband were in vain until he said that he would become a Christian if his troops overcame the Alemanni, who had crossed the Rhine. At the crisis of the battle, the king invoked Christ's help, promising to be baptised if he won the battle. The tide of the battle turned, and the Alemanni were defeated. Chlotildis sent for St Remigius to prepare the king for baptism, and he was baptised with three thousand of his warriors and many women and children. It is said that the chrism for the anointing was missing at the ceremony, but at the prayer of St Remigius a dove appeared carrying an ampoule of chrism in its beak (the dove and a phial of oil are his emblems). This was used in the consecration of the kings of

France until it was broken in the Revolution. A fragment, with its contents, is still preserved in Rheims cathedral. Under the protection of Clovis, Remigius carried on his work of conversion. Contemporary bishops, gathered for a conference at Lyons, describe him as having, 'everywhere destroyed the altars of the idols by a multitude of miracles and signs.' The saint was extremely tall (according to one tradition, seven feet in height), with a hook nose and a thick, tawny beard. His remains are preserved in the abbey of St Remy at Rheims. His feast day is 1 October.

Richard of Wych [c. 1197–1253]

St Richard, also known as **Richard of Chichester**, was born at Wych, now Droitwich, in Worcestershire, the younger son of a small landowner. His parents died when the children were young, and the estate fell into ruin because of the neglect of their guardian. Richard set to work and retrieved the family fortunes by his efforts, including manual labour. His brother wanted to make over the title deeds to him in gratitude and offered to arrange a wealthy marriage, but Richard turned his back on both suggestions and entered the University of Oxford as an almost penniless scholar. The following years were the happiest of his life, although he often had no food or firewood, and had to share a gown with two other students, which meant they attended lectures by a rota system. He began a lifelong friendship with the university chancellor, Edmund Rich, later St EDMUND. After Oxford, Richard went to Bologna to study canon law, staying there for seven years. He returned to Oxford and was appointed chancellor, but soon afterwards Edmund Rich, now archbishop of

Canterbury, made him his chancellor. Richard then devoted all his energies to helping the archbishop in the struggle between church and crown forced upon them by the financial malpractices of Henry III. Finally the archbishop retired to the Cistercian monastery at Potigny, ill and exhausted. Richard went with him and nursed him until his death. Richard then went into a Dominican house of studies in Orleans, where he stayed for two years and was ordained. He went back to England and worked as a parish priest in Deal until he was asked to resume his chancellorship by Boniface of Savoy, the new archbishop of Canterbury. In 1244 the see of Chichester became vacant, and Henry III secured the election of Robert Passelewe, a man whose practices, not all above board, had enriched the coffers of the king. The archbishop refused to confirm the election and nominated Richard to fill the see. The king refused to accept this ruling, and the case was taken to the pope, who decided in favour of Richard and consecrated him in 1245. But on returning to England, Richard found he was unable to enter his palace and was deprived of his lawful revenues. Henry also forbade anyone to give him lodgings or lend him money, so for two years Richard was a homeless wanderer in his own diocese. At last a priest, Simon of Tarring, took him into his house in a fishing village, and Richard administered from there for two years. He managed to hold synods in spite of his situation, and worked among fishermen and peasants. He enjoyed country pursuits and is said to have been skilled at pruning and grafting fruit trees. A fig orchard in the village of Hussey is said to have been raised from stock planted by Richard in the parsonage garden at Tarring. Under the threat of excommunication, Henry yielded to the pope and recognized Richard. He was now able to dispense hospitality, which he did very freely while keeping to very austere habits himself. Although much loved, he was a strict disciplinarian and felt strongly about nepotism, avoiding giving preference to any of his relatives. He quoted as an example Christ giving the keys of the kingdom to St Peter rather than to his cousin John. His last episcopal act was to consecrate a church at Dover to the memory of his great friend, St Edmund of Canterbury. He died in Dover and was buried in Chichester Cathedral near the altar of St Edmund. A lane near the cathedral is still called St Richard's Wynd. His feast day is 3 April.

Ringan *see* **Ninian**.

Robert Bellarmine [1542–1621]
St Robert, one of the most famous Catholic theologians, was born at Montelpulciano, near Siena in Italy. He entered the order of Jesuits in Rome in 1560 and studied theology at Padua and Louvain. Ordained priest in 1569, he was appointed the following year to the chair of theology at Louvain, but he returned to Rome in 1576 to lecture in the Roman College. In 1592 he became rector of the college and was made a cardinal in 1599 against his will. In 1602 he was made Archbishop of Capua. After the death of Pope Clement VIII, he managed to escape promotion to the papacy but was persuaded by Pius V to take an important role in the Vatican, where he stayed until his death. He was the church's chief defender at the time when its antagonists were strongest, in the sixteenth century. His feast day is 17 September.

S

Scholastica [died 548]

St Scholastica was the sister of St BENEDICT, and established herself in a convent near Monte Cassino. They met once a year on the mountainside at a spot near the abbey. The last time they met, Scholastica is said to have begged her brother not to leave her when night fell but to talk of the joys of heaven until the morning. Benedict refused, as it would be contrary to the rules of the monastery. Then a thunderstorm broke, which was so strong that it was impossible for him or his companions to leave. Scholastica told him that she had prayed to God, as her brother would not listen to her, and Benedict stayed with her, passing the night in spiritual conversation. Three days later he had a vision in which he saw Scholastica enter heaven in the form of a dove, and soon afterwards the news came that she had died. Her feast day is 10 February.

Sebastian [died 303]

St Sebastian was born at Narbonne in France, although his parents were natives of Milan and he was brought up there. He was a Christian but entered the army of Emperor Carinus in order to give secret help to the victims of the persecution. He became a tribune and commanded the first cohort at Milan. He helped many Christians, and also encouraged the resistance of some of the weaker members of the faith. Carinus was defeated and killed by Diocletian, who made Sebastian captain of a company of guards. But the persecution of the Christians was intensified, and he was denounced to the emperor who ordered him to be shot dead by arrows. He was taken to a field, pierced repeatedly with arrows and left for dead, but at night the widow of a martyr who went to bury him found him still alive. She took him home with her, tended his wounds and hid him until he was better, but he refused to flee. As soon as he was well enough, St Sebastian went to a place where he knew the emperor would be passing. He stood at the top of a staircase, saluted him and shouted, 'The words of thy priests are false, O Emperor, who say that we Christians are enemies of the State; for we do not cease to pray for thy welfare, and that of the realm.' Diocletian was infuriated and ordered Sebastian to be beaten to death with cudgels and his body thrown into a sewer. His feast day (with FABIAN) is 20 January.

Serf *see* **Kentigern**.

Simeon Stylites [died 460]
St Simeon Stylites was born in the village of Gesa, between Antioch and Cilicia, and as a boy kept his father's sheep. One day heavy snow forced him to leave them in the fold, and he went with his parents to church. There he heard the Beatitudes, and they changed his life. He sought advice and was told that the happiness promised could be obtained only by prayer, fasting and suffering and that these could be best practised in solitude. Simeon, who was thirteen years old, withdrew and prayed that God would show him the way to perfection of life. He had a dream in which he found himself

digging the foundations of a house. Every time he paused to rest, he was told to dig deeper until he had dug a pit that could contain the foundations of any building he could put up, however tall it might be. He went to a nearby monastery and lay at the gates for five days, until the abbot came out. Simeon told him, 'I long to be a servant of God and save my soul. Let me enter the monastery and do not send me away.' He was admitted and carried out menial tasks for two years. He then moved to the monastery of Heliodorus, where he increased his mortifications so much that the abbot dismissed him as a warning to the monks to avoid extremes. Then, in 423, he began to live on a pillar at Telanissus. At first the pillar was low, but over the years its height was increased to about sixty feet. On top was a platform with a balustrade, which was about twelve square feet. He spent the remaining years of his life there. After his death a monastery and sanctuary were built near the spot, and the base of Simeon's pillar can still be seen among the ruins. One reason for his extraordinary way of life was his need to get away from the people who flocked to him for prayers and advice. It was said, 'despairing of escaping the world horizontally, he tried to escape it vertically.' Of course the opposite happened, and even more people came to see him, from emperors downwards. The word Stylite was added to his name, from the Greek *stylos*, which means 'pillar'. His feast day is 5 January.

Simon [first century]

St Simon Zelotes, or the Canaanean, was one of the twelve disciples but very little is known about him. The words Zelotes and Canaanean both mean 'the zealous', but it is not clear if he belonged to the sect of the Zealots. The last biblical reference to him states that he received the Holy Ghost with his fellow Apostles. His emblem is a saw or a cross. His feast day (with JUDE) is 28 October.

Stephen [first century]
St Stephen was one of seven deacons appointed by the Apostles to relieve them of the routine duties of giving alms. He was distinguished by his faith and power and 'did great signs and wonders among the people.' His preaching brought him into conflict with the Hebraistic Jews, who argued with him but were unable to counter the wisdom and strength of his arguments. He was taken before the Sanhedrin and accused of prophesying the destruction of the temple and the passing of the Mosaic customs, superseded by the new covenant of Jesus Christ. We are told that everyone in the council, looking steadfastly at him, 'saw his face as it had been the face of an angel.' He gave a stirring speech of defence, asking which of the prophets had escaped persecution by the people. He then looked up to heaven and said he saw the glory of God and Jesus standing at his right hand. There was uproar, and Stephen was dragged out of the city and was stoned, his persecutors leaving their cloaks with Saul (*see* PAUL). He knelt down and shouted to God to forgive the people their sins, and died. In some parts of England, St Stephen's Day was known as 'wrenning day', from the custom of stoning wrens on that day in his memory. His feast day is 26 December.

Swithin [*c.* 805–862]
St Swithin, also known as **Swuthin**, was born in Wessex and sent at an early age to study grammar, philosophy and the

Holy Scriptures in the monastery of Winchester. He was ordained by Helmstan, bishop of Winchester, and Egbert, king of the West Saxons, made him his spiritual adviser. In 836 Ethelwulf succeeded his father and appointed Swithin to the see of Winchester, left vacant by Helmstan's death. St Swithin's influence restored communication with Rome, which had lapsed during the Danish invasions. He built and restored churches and built a bridge over the Itchen on the east side of Winchester. It was on this bridge that his one recorded miracle occurred. A poor woman, taking eggs to market, was jostled by a workman and dropped her basket. The eggs broke, but the bishop, who had seen what happened, was able to mend them. St Swithin was extremely humble and always went about on foot. He is said to have asked to be buried outside the church, where passers-by would walk on his grave and rain fall on it. This was done, and the grave gradually disappeared. It was rediscovered in the tenth century, and his remains were taken into the cathedral. No one can explain the famous rhyme about the his feast day:

> 'St Swithin's Day, if thou dost rain,
> For forty days it will remain;
> St Swithin's Day, if thou be fair,
> For forty days 'twill rain na' mair.'

One explanation is that the monks of Winchester, wishing to show honour to their saint, arranged to bring his remains into the church in defiance of his wishes. St Swithin, annoyed at this, caused rain to fall for forty days and nights so that they had to abandon their plan. He is invoked against drought. His feast day is 15 July.

T

Teresa of Avila [1515–1582]

St Teresa was a Spaniard who was born in Avila to devout noble parents. She had three sisters and nine brothers, one of whom was her special companion. When very small, they set off on a pilgrimage to the Moors, with the aim of being martyred and reaching heaven by a short road. They were amazed to read that the torments and glories of the next world were eternal, and liked to repeat the words 'for ever, for ever, for ever.' They made themselves hermitages in the garden, and when Teresa played with other little girls she loved to build monasteries. Afterwards, when her mother died, Teresa read romances, enjoyed choosing clothes, took an interest in her appearance and passed her time with frivolous friends. Her father was not pleased at this change and sent her to be educated in a convent under Augustinian rule, where she was influenced by the sister in charge who managed to remove 'the aversion I had felt to becoming a nun, an aversion which at one time was very great.' Before long Teresa had to leave because of her health, but the impressions were permanent, and when she was eighteen she decided to become a nun. Her father refused to give his consent, so she ran away from home and entered the Convent of the Incarnation at Avila, which belonged to the Carmelite order. For the first few years her health suffered, and she had to

171

leave the convent a few times. The convent belonged to a 'relaxed' order, which meant that the stringency of its rule had been relaxed by papal dispensations, and she found the rule too easy for the good of her soul and began to train herself in prayer. Earlier, the *Letters of Saint Jerome* had helped her decide on her vocation, and now she found *The Third Spiritual Alphabet* by Father Francis de Osuna a great help. But until she discovered the Jesuits, after being a nun for twenty years, she did not find a confessor who understood or helped her. The 'half-learned' and lenient did her most harm. She found concentration difficult and could not pray without a book. At one time she dreaded the hour when it was time to pray and would have preferred any penance. But she persisted and received favours in prayer and reached heights of spiritual ecstasy that made her one of the great mystics. Although her confessor admitted these mystical experiences were a sign of divine favour, he advised her to resist them. She struggled against them for two months but without success. Her visions are described by Teresa herself in her *Autobiography*, which she wrote at the command of her confessor. In spite of great opposition, Teresa founded a convent of strict, discalced (barefoot) nuns, dedicated to St JOSEPH, at Avila, on St Bartholomew's Day, 1562. She was outstanding as a practical reformer. She has been described as a doctor of the spiritual life, and her writings, *The Way of Perfection*, *Foundations* and *The Interior Castle*, are classics in the literature of mysticism. It was said of St Teresa that 'in twenty years she had filled Spain with monasteries, in which more than a thousand religious praise God.' She combined cheerfulness with mortification, and her spirit was transfused into

her nuns. It was said that they had 'turned the exercise of the
heroic virtue to a pleasant diversion.' She looked for intelligence even before piety in her novices, saying that an intelligent mind would see its faults and allow itself to be guided.
'May God preserve us from stupid nuns!' she said. Teresa
met with much opposition from those in authority. She died
at Alva while on a journey and was buried there. She was
declared patron saint of Spain during the Peninsular War, but
dethroned soon afterwards. Her feast day is 15 October.

Thaddaeus *see* **Jude**.

Theodore [*c.* 602–690]
In 667, Wighard, the archbishop elect of Canterbury, died in
Rome before consecration. Pope Vitalian nominated to the
vacant see a Greek monk from Tarsus in Cilicia, Theodore,
who was not yet a priest and over sixty years old. This sur-
prising appointment proved to be a resounding success. In
673 Theodore presided at the first council of the whole
church, at Hertford. The creation of new sees was one of his
main undertakings, and his achievements were largely in ecclesiastical organization, administration and discipline. He
found the church in England a disorganized missionary body
and left it a well-ordered province of the Catholic church,
looking to Canterbury as its metropolitan see. Theodore's
framework survived the upheavals of the sixteenth century
and is still the basis of the diocesan system of the Church of
England. Little is known of his personal character, but it can
be inferred that he was a man of great integrity because his
decisions were always regarded as very fair, and respected.
His feast day is 19 September.

Theresa of Lisieux [1873–1897]
The parents of Marie Francoise Thérèse were Louis Martin, a watchmaker, and his wife, Zélie Guérin, five of whose daughters became nuns. In 1888 Theresa entered the Carmelite convent of Lisieux in Normandy, where two of her sisters already were. She performed all the duties demanded of her by the austere Carmelite rule with great dedication and became assistant to the novice mistress when she was twenty-two. She considered volunteering for missionary work in Hanoi (now in Vietnam), and she is the patron saint of missionaries. But she contracted tuberculosis and died after eighteen months of heroic suffering. In her autobiography, *The Story of a Soul*, Theresa wrote that she would 'let fall a shower of roses'—in the form of miracles and favours—after her death. The book was published soon after her death and was an immediate and sensational success. Veneration for her became widespread, many miracles were attributed to her, and she was canonized in 1925, less than thirty years after her death. Her feast day is 1 October.

Thomas [first century]
St Thomas, also known as **Didymus**, both names meaning 'twin', was one of the twelve Apostles, and St JOHN records four of his sayings, which show his character as that of a man who was matter-of-fact and slow to believe but very loyal. When Lazarus lay dead and Jesus insisted on going to Bethany, in spite of the risks to his own life, St Thomas said, 'Let us also go that we might die with him.' When Jesus said, in his discourse in the upper chamber, 'Whither I go you know and the way you know,' St Thomas asked, 'Lord, we

know not whither thou goest, and how are we to know the way?' After the Resurrection, when the other disciples said, 'We have seen the Lord,' Thomas replied, 'Except I shall see in his hands the print of the nails and thrust my hand into his side, I shall not believe.' But when he saw Jesus the next Sunday, he exclaimed, 'My Lord and my God.' The Acts of Thomas relate that he went to India and preached. The story is that the missionary districts to which the Apostles would go were decided by casting lots. St Thomas drew India but objected, saying, 'I have not strength; I am weak. How can I, a Hebrew, teach the Indians?' In the night Jesus appeared to him and said, 'Fear not, Thomas; My grace is sufficient for thee.' But Thomas still protested and said, 'Whither Thou wilt, Lord, but not India.' While they were talking an Indian merchant in search of a skilful carpenter came up to them. Jesus said to him, 'Thou art looking for a carpenter. I have a slave for sale well skilled in the craft of a carpenter,' and sold Thomas for twenty pieces of silver. So he was taken to India where he worked as a carpenter, preached, and was eventually martyred at Mylapore. The Malabar Christians regard him as their Apostle to this day, and when St Francis Xavier preached in India, he found memorials to Thomas. His patronage of architects is based on the story, in the Acts of Thomas, that an Indian king gave Thomas a large sum of money to build a palace for which he had drawn up plans. But Thomas spent the money on the poor, so building the king a palace in heaven. His feast day is 3 July.

Thomas Aquinas [1226–1274]
St Thomas has been described as the most learned of the

saints and the most saintly of the learned. He was born near Aquino, in Italy. His father belonged to a distinguished family, descended from the Lombards, and his mother was of aristocratic Norman origin. His parents intended him to be the abbot of the rich and powerful Benedictine Abbey of Monte Cassino, and sent him to be educated there at the age of five. He stayed there for seven years, and when he came home he acted as his father's almoner during a famine at Loreto. He is said on one occasion to have filled his cloak with bread for the poor and, when challenged by his father, to have opened it and let drop a shower of roses. At thirteen he entered the University of Naples, where he studied the arts and sciences. At Naples he began to worship at the Church of the Order of Preachers. As he prayed there, the brothers sometimes saw rays of light shining above his head. At the age of nineteen he was received into the Dominican order, without the consent of his parents, who had wanted him to become a Benedictine. When they learned that he had joined a mendicant order his mother, Theodora, followed him from Naples to Rome to try and make him change his mind. Thomas was already on his way to Bologna, but his brothers caught up with him and took him home by force, and he was imprisoned in a nearby castle for two years. In 1245 his family resigned themselves to the inevitable, and Thomas was allowed to return to his order. The Dominicans sent him to Cologne to study under Albertus Magnus, but at first neither his teacher nor his companions recognized his abilities. He was called 'the dumb Sicilian ox', but one day he defended a thesis with such skill that his master said, 'We call this youth "dumb ox", but the day will come when the whole world will resound with his bellowing.' Thomas was appointed professor at the Dominican school in Cologne, and in 1252 was sent to Paris to teach in the University, receiving his doctorate four years later. He returned to Italy for nine years to preach and to teach in a school attached to the papal court. In 1261 he went to Rome at the invitation of Pope Urban IV, and soon afterwards began the *Summa Theologica*, which was to contain the whole of the Christian religion from the existence of God to the precepts of morality, with every conceivable objection stated and answered. It occupied the last nine years of his life but was never finished. Not long before he died, St Thomas had a vision while celebrating Mass and refused to write any more. When asked the reason for this he replied, 'I cannot, for everything I have written seems worthless by the side of what I have seen.' Thomas became ill on a journey to Lyons and was taken to the Benedictine Abbey of Fessa-Nuova, where he died. He is the patron saint of all universities, colleges and schools. His body lies at Toulouse, in the cathedral of Saint-Sernin. His feast day is 28 January.

Thomas Becket [1118–1170]

Thomas, also known as **Thomas of Canterbury**, was the son of a prosperous Norman sheriff of London. By the time he was twenty-two he had lost both his parents and had to work for his living in commercial offices in London. When he was twenty-four Thomas was appointed to the household of Theobald, archbishop of Canterbury, where his energy and charm gained him rapid promotion. King Henry II himself recognized his qualities. Thomas soon became an archdea-

con, and it was by his intervention in Rome that Pope
Eugenius III ruled against Stephen's son Eustace as a successor to the throne of England, making Henry's title secure.
The friendship between the king and Thomas grew and, at
thirty-six, Thomas was appointed chancellor. When Thomas
travelled as Henry's ambassador, the splendour of his entou-
rage dazzled his hosts. In support of the king's war in France,
Thomas led his own men to Toulouse and rode at the head of
seven hundred knights. In 1161 Archbishop Theobald died,
and Thomas was the obvious successor. With amazing fore-
sight, he told Henry, 'Should God permit me to be archbishop of Canterbury I should soon lose your Majesty's favour, and the affection with which you honour me would be
changed into hatred.' But Henry would take no refusal, and
Thomas was consecrated. Against the king's wishes he gave
up the office of chancellor and all the trappings of secular authority. He wore a hair shirt under his cassock. But conflict
between the Church and the court grew as the archbishop
made it plain to the king that he would never surrender the
integrity of the Church, insisting that those who served it
should be ruled by ecclesiastical law. At the Council of
Clarendon it became clear that the king would be content
with nothing less than the surrender of the Church's right to
appeal to the pope. A number of bishops aligned themselves
with the king. Relations between Thomas and the king grew
so stormy that Thomas set sail for France where Pope Alexander III rebuked him for having temporized as far as he had.
The king confiscated the lands of those who had supported
Thomas and told them to join him in exile. Thomas entered
the abbey of St Columba as the guest of King Louis VII of

France. He regarded the six years he spent in France as a spiritual retreat. At last Henry himself came to see Thomas, and they met in Normandy and agreed to bury the past. But Thomas had no illusions and told the bishop of Paris, 'I am going to England to die.' Back home, after a triumphal welcome, Thomas refused to lift the ban of excommunication from the intransigent bishops whose denial of the Church's cause he had never condoned. At Bur, King Henry spoke the words that some of his hearers took as a mandate for the assassination of Thomas Becket. Four knights: Reginald Fitzurse, William de Tracy, Hugh de Morville and Richard le Breton, set off from Bur, believing they had the king's authority. On 19 December 1170 they went to his cathedral as vespers were being sung, terrifying the monks, who closed the door against them. But Thomas himself threw back the door and let them in. The knights tried to drag him from the sacred building, but he shouted, 'I am ready to die, but God's curse be on you if you harm my people.' William de Tracy struck him with his sword, and Richard le Breton severed the top of his head. It is recorded that thunder crashed over the cathedral and, as the murderers escaped, it echoed all over Europe as news of the murder spread. Thomas was canonized in 1174, and his body was put in a shrine behind the high altar in 1220. Canterbury became the most popular place of pilgrimage in Christendom until it was rifled and its relics burned by Henry VIII in 1538. His feast day is 29 December

Thomas More [1478–1535]

Thomas More's father was a judge, and after two years at Oxford, Thomas was admitted as a student at Lincoln's Inn, being called to the bar in 1501. In 1504 he entered Parliament. In the following year he married Jane Colt, and they had three sons and a daughter, but his wife died when young, and Thomas then married a widow, Alice Middleton, who could be a mother to his young children. Thomas was a humanist and a reformer, 'a gentleman of great learning, both in law, art and divinity.' He was also an extremely witty man. Among his close friends were Bishop Fisher and the man he called 'Erasmus my darling'. By 1516 Thomas had written his great work, *Utopia*. He filled a succession of high posts under King Henry VIII, and in 1529 was appointed lord chancellor. As a judge he was famous for his fairness and incorruptibility. But when his career and reputation were at their height, King Henry demanded that his marriage to Catherine of Aragon should be annulled. Thomas was a close friend of the king, but he believed the marriage to be valid and in 1532 resigned the chancellorship and retired from public life. In 1534, with Bishop Fisher, he refused to take an oath that involved the repudiation of papal religious authority, and he was committed to the Tower of London. During his fifteen months' imprisonment he wrote a *Dialogue of Comfort against Tribulation*. Thomas More was tried on a charge of treasonably denying the king's supreme headship on earth of the Church of England, found guilty and sentenced to death. He told the court that he could not act against his conscience and hoped that 'We may yet hereafter in Heaven merrily all meet together to everlasting salvation.' He was beheaded on Tower Hill, telling the crowd that he was 'the king's good servant—but God's first.' His feast day is 22 June.

U

Ursula [fourth century]
It is said that Ursula was the daughter of the king of Cornwall and that her hand was sought in marriage by a neighbouring prince. Not wishing to marry, she asked if, before the wedding, she could travel for three years with eleven thousand maidens as her companions. Her request was granted, and they set sail on eleven galleys. A storm drove their ships up the Rhine to Cologne, and on to Basle. They crossed the Alps on a pilgrimage to Rome, but on their return journey they were massacred by the Huns. St Ursula became the patron saint of schoolgirls and their teachers. Her emblem is a pilgrim's staff with the Christian banner of victory (a red cross on a white background). Her feast day is 21 October.

V

Valentine [died 270]

St Valentine was a Roman priest who was imprisoned during the reign of Claudius II for assisting his fellow Christians throughout the persecution. He refused to renounce his faith, was beaten with clubs and beheaded. The custom of sending valentines on 14 February is probably not connected with this saint; the name Valentine was not unusual at this period. It is more likely that it arose from the very old belief that this was the day on which birds chose their mates. His feast is 14 February.

Venerable Bede *see* Bede.

Vincent [died 304]

St Vincent was born in Saragossa, in Spain, and educated by the bishop of Saragossa, Valerius. The persecution of the Church was growing at this time and Dacian, the Roman governor of Spain, arrested Vincent and Valerius and imprisoned them at Valencia. They were kept for a long time in a state of semi-starvation, and when they were finally brought in front of the proconsul they were alternately threatened and tempted. Vincent, answering on behalf of them both because Valerius had a speech impediment, said that they were ready to suffer for the true God. Valerius was banished, but Vincent was returned to prison and tortured. With spiritual help the saint kept his resolve. He was thrown into his cell, whose floor was covered in broken earthenware, but his guard, looking through a crack in the door, saw the cell filled with light and Vincent walking with angels, and was himself converted to Christianity. After this, Dacian is said to have relented and to have handed the saint over to his friends, but he died almost immediately. His body was thrown into the sea, but it was washed up and given a Christian burial. It was later buried under the altar of the main church at Valencia. His feast day is 22 January.

Vincent de Paul [1576–1660]

St Vincent de Paul was a Gascon, born at Puoy near Bayonne. His father was a peasant farmer and he was the third child in a family of four sons and two daughters. He was sent to be educated by the Franciscans at Dax, near his home, and later studied at Toulouse and was ordained at the age of twenty. He went to Paris and was appointed one of the chaplains of Margaret de Valois. In Paris Vincent met a priest, Peter de Bérulle, who persuaded him to become chaplain and tutor to the household of Philip de Gondi, count of Joigny. The de Gondi family was deeply religious. Vincent stayed with them for nineteen years, and it was from this association that the works of charity with which he is associated grew. With the de Gondi family's approval, Vincent began to preach in the church at Folleville, drawing such huge crowds of penitents that he had to call on the Jesuits to help him. Apart from one short interval, he stayed in the de Gondi household until

1632, when he moved to the priory of Saint-Lazare, where he stayed until his death. During this time he began to preach parochial missions and encouraged others to do the same. He founded the first unenclosed Order of Sisters of Mercy, which was to devote itself to active work among the poor by teaching and nursing. Vincent never forgot his peasant origins, and loved the tough souls (*les âmes cailleuses*) of working people. But he did not despise the rich. He gathered them, men and women, into his Confraternity of Charity and set them to work visiting hospitals and the homes of the poor. Allied to this were the Sisters of Charity. Rich women were enlisted as Ladies of Charity to collect funds and work for good causes. He found that the preparation of candidates for the priesthood was sadly neglected, so he established retreats for ordinands that were held at Saint-Lazare, at first four times, and then six times a year. They each lasted two weeks, and seventy to ninety ordinands were present at each. Finding them so successful, Vincent started retreats for laymen of all kinds. He called Saint-Lazare his Noah's Ark, because all sorts of animals were lodged there. 'This house,' he said, 'was formerly used as a retreat for lepers; they were received here, and not one was cured: now it is used to receive sinners, who are sick men covered with spiritual leprosy, but are cured by the grace of God.' Hundreds of babies were abandoned in Paris every year. Once Vincent saw a man mutilating a baby for begging purposes. Moved with pity, he established a foundling hospital and is said to have wandered about the slums of Paris, bringing back deserted babies wrapped in his cloak. One of his last great works was to help found and organize a vast workhouse for the destitute people of Paris. He visited galleys and prisons and ministered to the convicts who were treated with great brutality by the state and neglected by the Church. He is said, on seeing a young convict in tears, to have taken his place and served for a time in a galley. St Vincent was canonized in 1737, and in 1885 was proclaimed patron of all charitable societies by Pope Leo XIII. He is often depicted in a black cassock with a knotted girdle, holding a baby or young child in his arms, sometimes with a Sister of Mercy kneeling at his feet. His feast day is 27 September.

W

Wilfrid [634–709]

Wilfrid was a Northumbrian of noble birth. He was educated at Lindisfarne, and became infected with a love both for learning and the monastic life. He travelled to Canterbury and then to Rome. In Rome Wilfrid abandoned Celtic customs and adhered to those of Rome. He spent three years at Lyons on his way home. King Oswy of Northumbria approved of the Roman observance of the date of Easter (a week earlier than that of the Scots or Celtic usage), and he installed Wilfrid as abbot of a monastery at Ripon. Wilfrid introduced the rule of St BENEDICT in the community and was shortly afterwards ordained priest by the bishop of the West Saxons. To end the dispute about Easter, Oswy summoned the Synod of Whitby, at which the Roman party, of which Wilfrid was a prominent supporter, was victorious. He was appointed to the see of York. As archbishop of York, Wilfrid restored the cathedral, went about the diocese on foot, and introduced the use of the Roman chant. Unfortunately, he fell out with King Egfrid, who succeeded Oswy. Ethelreda, Egfrid's wife, wanted to enter the religious life and had for ten years refused to consummate her marriage. Wilfrid took her part and helped her enter a convent. The diocese of York

was then divided into four by St Theodore, and three more
bishops consecrated. Wilfrid set out for Rome to put his case
before the pope, but was shipwrecked and driven on to the
coast of Frisia for a while. When he at last arrived back in
England and showed Egfrid the papal decree that declared
that he should be restored to his see, the king said it was a
forgery and imprisoned him for nine months. When Wilfrid
was released, he went to Sussex and converted almost the
whole pagan province, encouraged by King Ethelwalh, who
had recently been baptised. He averted famine by teaching
the people to catch fish, when previously they had caught
only eels. The king gave him land at Selsey, where he settled
and established a monastery. In 686 Wilfrid was restored to
Ripon by Alcfrid, Egfrid's successor, but within five years he
had quarrelled with him and was again banished. For some
years he filled the vacant see at Lichfield until a new archbishop of Canterbury decreed that he should resign and return to Ripon. He set out for Rome once more to appeal, this
time in his seventieth year. King Alcfrid, on his deathbed,
repented of the injustices done to Wilfrid. The saint took pos-
session of the diocese of Hexham. In 709 Wilfrid visited all
the monasteries that he had founded in Mercia. He died at
Oundle and was buried at Ripon in the church of St Peter.
Wilfrid was the first Englishman to carry a lawsuit to the
Roman courts. The saint had an aptitude for making enemies and a genius for making friends. He was also a crea-
tive artist who knew how to create splendid effects through
art and religious ceremonial. Above all, his ruling passion
was the service of God and his Church. His feast day is 12
October.

Wulfstan [1009–1095]

Wulfstan, the son of a Warwickshire thane, was the last of the Anglo-Saxon saints. He was educated in the monasteries of Evesham and Peterborough, and became a monk at Worcester. As prior of the house, he restored its fortunes, religious and temporal, and was noted for his pastoral activity, and in 1062 was made bishop of Worcester. After the Norman conquest he supported King William I and was allowed to retain his diocese. He fought the slave trade in Bristol, preaching to the traders in their own language. He enforced the discipline of priestly celibacy (a difficult task in those days) and built new churches, also restoring his cathedral at Worcester. He practised a monastic regime, often spending whole nights before the altar in prayer, and ate and drank in extreme moderation. It was said that one day, when serving late High Mass and very hungry, he was distracted by the smell of roast goose drifting in from the kitchens. It made it so hard for him to concentrate that he took a vow to abstain from meat and firmly adhered to it. He was not a learned man, but he was remarkable for the purity of his life and the power of his preaching, with many of his sermons moving his listeners to tears. His feast day is 19 January.